Steel

Black

we are ~~steal~~ steel ~~still~~ HERE

aj houston

Not Just Alphabets

Steel Black

Not Just Alphabets Publishing

Las Vegas, Nevada

All Not Just Alphabets Publishing titles, AJ Houston, wordart, imprints and lines distributed are available at special quantity discounts for bulk purchases for sales promotion, fund raising, premiums, educational, institutional and library use.

Copyright © 2021 by AJ Houston. All rights reserved.

No part of this work may be reproduced or transmitted in any form or by any means, electronic or mechanical, including photocopying and recording, or by any information storage retrieval system without the prior written permission of A.J. Houston or Not Just Alphabets. Email notjustalphabets@gmail.com address to Permissions.

Printed in the U. S. A.

Library of Congress Catalog Card Number:

ISBN: 978-1-7338810- 4- 3

Steel

Black

we are ~~steal~~ steel ~~still~~ HERE

aj houston

Copyright © 2021 AJ Houston/ Not Just Alphabets

Steel Black

Introduction

Let us start here

Twenty-Twenty had such great anticipation, held so much promise before its arrival. It arrived lifeless; the fuse was wet couldn't light it if all of us tried. I would prefer not to write with such specificity when it comes to dates and time because Hind Sight is such a rude person to meet. 'Steel Black', I hope means exactly what and how it sounds. First and foremost we are 'Still' here after hundreds of years of torture, executions, rape, murder, human experiment's, it would be appropriate to add anything else of horror that can happen to a people transitioning from slavery, mental incarceration and are now supposed to be free.

The other 'Steal' is in direct reference to the fact, most of the inventions by people of color throughout history are somehow not listed in their names under the patents registered. Also included in the line of stolen items looks, lips, hips, breast size, waist, hair texture, hair styles, skin color, fashion and clothes all stolen or rather borrowed without receipts for returning any of the items to its rightful owner. For the titles reference 'Steel', mainly because protect and serve are constantly shooting unarmed Black men in backs, fronts, sides, wherever bullets go when directed or aimed. Imagining lead can't penetrate melanin, as if Black men have skin made of Steel. As if all the deaths or murders are from lead poisoning.

If you add centuries of pain to years survived, multiply exponentially by body count. (include estimates in unmarked graves, planted on plantations for soil replenishing, burned after hanging, missing, taken, murdered and disfigured.) Be advised there is no mathematical equation able to compute the loss of Black lives suffered in the colonies or these fifty so called states. America has created new ways for subtracting us from its numbers. Nevertheless, we are still here, steal here, steel here... Still Black, Steal Black, Steel Black.

-Steel Black-

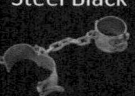

Steel Black

criminals by color, sentenced by melanin

There were many different chains used for departure and upon arrival to a new shore. We were treated as criminals before capture. Here we are centuries later still wearing sin for skin. Still treated as guilty before any crime has been committed. Imagine we removed the chains from our harrowed history and began to treat each other as family. It wouldn't matter what outsiders thought or how they treated us, if we all had our own backs.

history is supposed to be the written version of the truth

rediscover the truth for yourself. Know thy self

is demanding you to know your history

-aj houston-

Steel Black

Table of Content

Dedication	15
My Prayer	16
Black Is Black	19
Now And Then	23
Hope	29
Coffee	33
A Letter To My Grandfather	37
Black Girl	41
Broken	44
Amen	49
Better Self	54
Centuries of Mis Understanding	57
Distraction	61
Family	63

The Devil's Hand	67
Harriet's Feet	71
Dear Covid - 19	75
The Negro Can Dance	78
Fingers Never Stop Talking	81
Lesson On Marches	86
A Little Note	89
Essay "The Inhumanity Clause"	93
I Dream In Revolutions	99
Dixie	103
White Out	105
Black Bodies Black Bullets Black Dreams	106
My Next Workshop	109
Rest	111
What Is It Worth	115
Essay: How Dreams Look Close Up	119

Steel Black

Trust Ink	123
Breathing	126
Confessions of an Ink Pen in Witness Protection	129
Lost In Time	133
In the Garden of Cotton	136
Dressing for Church	139
Five Generations from Here	144
Water	147
Wanna Write No Mo	151
Wake Up	155
Come Mourning	158
Fractured Mindset	160
History Updated	163
They Told Me Lies	167
The River	170
How To Build An Underground Railroad	174

Promises	179
Inheritance	183
Just Answers	188
Keepsakes	190
Lessons in Sound	193
Maybe It's Just Me	197
Love Poem	204
Monuments	208
No Not One	213
Sunshine and Rain	216
What Hate Looks Like	220
The Air They Un Promised Us	222
Muddy Water	224
Crowns	229
We The People	231
Home	236

Steel Black

Unforgiven	240
Rise	244
This Is Why Death Sounds So Familiar III	247
Imagination and Apologies	249
Be Careful	251
Envy	253
Play Me Some Jazz	255
Speaker Tax	257
The Messenger	260
Dear Martin, I Have A Dream	265
Burdens	269
Wide Open	272
When I Grow Up	274
They Make Me Nervous	277
End of the Road	279
America, I Am So So Sorry	280

Thank You   285

Media Pages   286

About the Author   287

Preview of Published Works   288

Thank You for your support, it is the art and artist continuing to build a better nation, country, world. Support free thought.

Thank You

aj houston

Steel Black

Dedication

to every step marched, every sign handwritten, painted and drawn, to every life lost, taken, to every name we shall forever repeat, to every face we cannot forget, to every father missing his sons and daughters for whatever reason, to Justice may she arrive on time or may she get here soon. This book is dedicated to my mother Birdie, father Jimmie Jay, Myrtle, Jahmal, Rev Conner I, Geneva. Oretha, R.T., Booker, Cedrick, Fredrick, my daughters, sons, grandchildren, cousins, Aunts, Uncles, brother and sisters. To everyone I have met, talked to, interviewed, spit a poem with, heard a poem from. To love, life and to the love of my life F. Marie... thank you all for everything.

-aj houston-

Steel Black

My Prayer

some days I start my prayer

you know, yesterday wasn't that bad

I passed four different police on the highway

looked them in their eyes and made it home safe

thank you for safe passage

other days I pray, Lord I'm tired

tired of asking you to give peace

to families whose child was taken

took their last breath on a street

not far from home, not by accident

almost taken the same way each time

taken because he looked like me

it is as if I pray in color

I don't know how white prayers sound

I pray in brown and black grace

ask for black and brown blessings

some days I pray like Martin

let justice roll down like a mighty stream

too afraid this whole country

will be washed away in the flood

you don't know how hard black men pray

some days I pray in thunder

tears wailing as if these eyes are home for storms

fist balled up banging on the wind

as if pearly gates stood right there

at the next turn, next step

next exit, next stop sign, next breath

I pray in motion while the car is still moving

pray coming out of the grocery store

out of the gas station, out of seven eleven

pray leaving my mother's house

you don't know how hard black men pray

how hard it is to ask the same thing every day

can I just make it to the next street

can you give me safe passage home

I want to see my family

can you place a hedge around my sons

Lord just let them be

can my daughters sleep in peace

I pray they double check the address

pray they no longer serve warrants after midnight

pray their trigger finger gets arthritis

pray no new black boy fits the description

pray I'm not dressed like someone

Not Just Alphabets

Steel Black

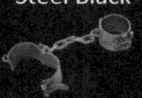

who committed a crime in another state

you don't know how hard black men got to pray

I got to pray for me and you, for them, for us

pray for those I know and don't know

some days I am praying the whole day

like it is a job, a business, a mission

like it's a goal, like my ancestors made me do it

like there is a bandage around my voice

and it is a safe day for black passage

I know somebody got to do it

you don't know how hard

my mother and grandmother had to pray

just for me to get this far, so I could write

so I could pray these prayers

you don't know how hard it is

to ask the same thing every day

maybe God is everywhere

I hope he sees this skin I wear is a problem

for this country, for law enforcement

for justice, for freedom

I will keep praying like it is my job

my mission, my purpose, my poetry

I just hope heaven is listening

Black is Black

I've grown tired of coughing

blood apologies for blatant attacks

on darkness - you believe this skin

makes us family

means we know anyone

who bares the same hue

your failure to label black

as everything but human

is cause for our any means necessary

for dreams differed

for our fear of the color blue

I've grown sick regurgitating I'm sorry's

for breathing the same air

using the same bathrooms

attending the same schools

drinking from the same fountains

when will enough be enough

how many bodies does it take

before you call it murder

before you hold accountable

those undeserving to protect us

Steel Black

you probably believe this is just a poem

for black history month those 28 days

we discover all the things

you hoped we would never find

we need a new language

one to use without regret

able speak it without singing

able to sing without humming the chorus

without reminders of cotton

will not need to be accompanied

by drums and dancers

without building railroads in spirituals

without blazing underground paths

in secret verses

I see you hiding behind a false sense

of political correctness

we will no longer cover your prejudices

in sheep's clothing

I keep praying for an executive order

an amendment, a new addition to the constitution

that doesn't need sixty votes

for ratification - will not be faced

with the scrutiny of this injustice system

I see your white wigs each time you convene

echoes of your fathers and grandfathers

prejudice in your sentences

your tongue weighs as heavy

as a ton of cane or fifty gallons of molasses

there is no sweet in your sour

no you in your just us

here we are hundreds of years removed

from being removed

you may not remember

banning our language, changing our names

insuring we fit whatever description

required for us to be subservient

there are niggaz on back order

in the manuals passed down

from your grandfather's father

we still march to dismembered rhythms

to the awkward melody of flash bangs, tear gas

peppered bullets are a sign we are on the right path

it is easy to forget how long this struggle has lasted

our fingers built this place

front line in every war

back seat on every bus

Not Just Alphabets

Steel Black

we've been here. built here,

bled here, died here, live here

when will enough be enough

how many bodies does it take

before you call it murder

I born American, will die American

but still fighting for the right

to be American

Now and Then

on September 15, 1955

the picture on the cover

of Jet Magazine should have changed the world

back then we were still asking America

to give us what she promised

or a little empathy, some of that compassion

she keeps bottled up until pain gets too heavy to bear

I would never ask my mother what she thought of now

every week same story, every day the same story

every year same story, we can divide

the weeks and days by her age

and see how many stories she has had to bear

I did not think of it this way in the beginning

by now, she would have a house filled with t-shirts

with the faces of black babies, black people

unarmed, unaware of when their last day of breath would be

how many street corners, corner stores,

drive through fast food, alleys, how many stories

can we tell in our communities

of unsolicited confrontations with protect and serve

I am guessing, there are Klansmen wearing police blue

Steel Black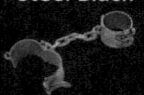

in graveyards digging up old leaders

praying they find a note, a letter

not completely decayed, a message in a bottle

America must create new excuses for these

closed eye sessions, once upon a time

there was this place called land of the free

where huddled masses would go, there are still

stories in books of their trouble getting here

arriving with two dollars and fifteen cents

just the clothes on their backs - hiding in luggage

as ship's cargo does not matter how

the plan was to get here

once a shore there were chances

golden opportunities

they were given land, animals and feed

you know the humanity starter kit

then came these people - let us call it came

not took or stolen, were not actually willing participants

not given boarding passes, were not allowed

a carrying bag, suitcase or drum

were not told how long, to where, for what,

did not know the captain's name or origin

did not know if it was the Jesus or the Clotilda

didn't know what race they were or what race

borrowed them from the soil they had

grown accustomed to, I do not think groups

of people were broken into races at this juncture

in his story, upon arrival, let's call it parted

from our kinsman, not beaten, not separated

not sold, let's call it bartered for cash

lets just say we were all strippers on stages

butt naked for public viewing

then came this now

don't think they were ready for this new way

of communicating, of taking moving pictures

got too use to one story one truth

turning off body cameras so lies fit well

in the scriptures written by blue angels

on police reports

I would never ask my mother what she thought of now

most Americans still struggle to get over then

get over America assassinating King and Malcom

there are no more gospel songs to give happy feet

to us downtrodden mourners

no more tears available for release

 it is not that we don't cry no more

Steel Black

we are empty - dry eyes will not let us not see

we cannot afford to sleep, America never sleeps

keep planning how to get rid of us

yeah of us, niggaz, immigrants, Mexicans who belong here

other dark skin, brown skin, tan skin people who belong here

there are plans to hush us, separate us from the almost free

we have yet to see - plans to get rid of our ability to vote

freedom of choice, freedom of speech, our freedom of religion

freedom to assemble, freedom to protest

it no longer seems as if these freedoms are still free

maybe like Mamie Till asked Mr. Rainer for a hammer

we should ask America for the same

give us a hammer to open this crate of privilege

we need to reveal the ugly you have spent

years trying make pretty

it is past time we divulge this racism

that has been on lock down

show the world America's most harrowed secret

the systematic approach of regression

congress keeps a schedule of how to hide free

from a people in destress for more than four hundred years

or maybe we can go backyard barbecuing with forty-five

ninety-nine years after Klansmen bombed

Black Wallstreet in Tulsa have a beer

toast some moonshine at his white hood rally

on Juneteenth, share some ribs

two hundred and fifty-five years after

General Granger showed up late with some

free on his lips, some "remain quietly at their present homes

and work for wages, know this for sure they will not

be supported in idleness either there or elsewhere"

we do not get whole messages anymore

do not quite know how to listen when they come

I am not sure if those who profess to be woke

believe their community, their nation needs them to vote

whenever elections show up unnoticed

you must be sleep, mentally deficient

if you forget to register

my mother taught me to vote at first chance

we should not inquire to doctors

why her movement has slowed

why her back hurts, why she stops

and cries every now and then

they will say it is osteo-whatever or scolio-something

they will not tell you black women carry on their shoulders

pain of generations, the struggle of a continent

Steel Black

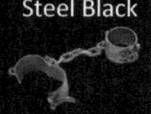

their backs are weighed down

from too many tombstones

too many babies, boys, men

women gone too soon

I do not mean to be long winded

it has been too long

since we had a moment to breathe

without a boot, knee or hands around our necks

this is the breath we have been needing

the air they un promised us years ago

I would never ask my mother what she thought of now

I can still see then in the arthritis in her fingers

from clutching memories she will not speak of

the swelling of her ankles, the pain in her knees

she will say, "I'm kicking but not high

each of these ins and outs is grace from a God

that would never give us more than we can bear"

she would say this now is then and this then is now

and from where she sits ain't no difference at all

Hope

to anyone who responds 'all lives matter' after hearing 'Black Lives Matter'

who knew the day would come

when Hope had to choose sides, choose a color

the choice of loud or soft, big or little

I have heard a little Hope goes a long way

we been Hoping long enough

been Hoping before they called it Hope

wishing before they called it wishing too

we keep Hoping for Hope to mean

something other than us just Hoping

maybe we were white Hoping

today, I am asking Hope to choose a color

maybe add some doves they are supposed to be

a symbol for peace, ask the doves to choose a color

everything can't be white, justice can't stay blind

justice's blindfold is white maybe it should be black too

I think she can see through it, watch us in the courts

on the streets, watch us get pulled over

watch us get choked, shot, beat

she still be quiet, ain't spoke up

Not Just Alphabets

Steel Black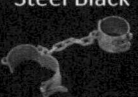

since they placed that sword in her hands

holding scales that look balanced

justice for us is an unbalancing act we ain't good at

got two left thumbs, can't juggle fairness and opportunity

when they cannot seem to find where we live

guess they are waiting for change, waiting for gentrification

what if Hope were black would Black Lives Matter then

would the echo remain all lives matter

as if they are killing y'all at random too

when your son or daughter leaves home

your only worry is will they come back by curfew

Black Lives Matter means

we want to have the same worry

don't want to have to download an app

created just for a video and audio report

when police stop anyone black

one push of a button can record your own suicide

by the hands of your protector

what if Hope were black would it stop us from seeing color

would it make our neighborhoods safe

there are three fingers pointing back at us

when we use one to show blame

we are three times at fault, when we don't discuss

the crime on our own streets, don't speak of shootings

fail to condemn murder by proxy by color

could it stop this black on black, curtail self-destruction

we haven't protected our black women since way back

since massah came and took her as we watched

couldn't do a thing about it, even now we are still watching

when we gone talk to each other like therapy

like we trying to fix this broken we keep breaking

we are marching for truth and justice

and do not offer truth or justice in our own community

marching for rights outside of where we live

but where we live it ain't right

the way we treat our brothers and sisters

ain't even listening to ourselves, cannot hear our own demands

what if Hope were black, could it stand guard on corners

be like watchmen at midnight, would it tell the truth

when we step out of line

when we break the laws in our community

we need black laws in our own community

maybe the police would not need to visit so often

yeah, I said it

I want black hope, black doves, black laws, black justice

a black mask around a black lady justice's eyes

Steel Black

want this black on black to cease

we need black on black to mean

we are blacks buying black

we are placing black dollars

at the forefront of our community

imagine if Hope were black

would Black Lives Matter then

we need black lives to matter

just as much as white lives

saying all lives matter makes no sense

until Black Lives Matter too

maybe Hope should be black

with a host of black doves

I have heard doves are a

perfect symbol for peace

it should not matter

if the doves white or black

Coffee

a good picker can pick somewhere

between 100 to 200 pounds of coffee per day

imagine how difficult it must have been

to pick your purchase through seven layers of skin

melanin has to be the hardest

substance to see through

light, dark, brown, tan, chocolate

coffee is packed and shipped in jute bags

a natural fiber made from the outer stem

and skin of a jute plant

slaves were packed and shipped in bags of skin

the natural covering given by the most high

necessary to keep our muscles intact

and our bones warm

sixty-nine kilograms compared to

one hundred and fifty-two pounds

it only matters how close they were

when forced into the cargo hull of whatever vessel

used to transport them to a new shore

how can you tell the difference

between black coffee and black bodies

Steel Black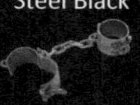

when they are both shipped the same way

coffee is said to be the best part of waking up

slaves were waking up before the best part of the day

before Folgers, Starbucks, Maxwell House

before darkness, before day, before time was ripe

someday soon, very soon America will have

an equal amount of weight in black coffee and black bodies

consumed per year by the populous and police

no justice, no justice we have to wonder if peace

has ever been a naturalized citizen

ever visited these shores with the intent of staying

if peace even remained after the smoke of canons cleared

after the last sword was sheathed, last musket fired

the last revolution, final separation

of church and state, the waving white flag

between the confederates and north

after hate and hangings, after whites only

fear of blacks voting, separation of black men and family

it is always shoot, kill, investigate, vacation

shoot, kill, investigate, vacation

how many shots, how many bullets does it take

for a round trip to your favorite island

favorite foreign escape, favorite cruise

no justice, no justice - America don't do peace

at least not in the same sentence with black

negro, African american, colored, nigga

the best coffee comes from the same region

supposedly the best free labor came from

we consume in this country one hundred

and forty-six million cups of coffee per year

which is closely equivalent to the number

of years being served consecutively

by innocent black men and women

American found guilty while innocence

blatantly stared them in the face

how do you like your coffee

black, cream, sugar, honey

sugar substitute, there are no substitutes

for missing sons and fathers

ain't no sweet in taking innocent lives

most police like their coffee black with ice

that way the blood doesn't flow

death and murder can be so messy sometimes

most police like their coffee

warm poured slowly

in the middle of streets and parking lots

Not Just Alphabets

Steel Black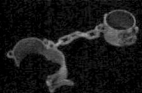

like their coffee pressed hard against knees

ground deep into sidewalks, concrete

seven shots in the back

cold with little or no movement

like their blacks in the clouds

or hidden six feet under dirt

like their coffee severed from the vine

ripped from the family tree it came from

imagine wasting a hot cup of coffee

on your clean white shirt

some stains are not removable

fresh blood on a clean blue uniform

blood spilt on cell phone video

you can't get that shit off

have you ever asked yourself

where does the billions of dollars go

in an industry that makes so much

you have to wonder how a conversation

about coffee can transport us to color

race, culture, profits, to a hood

with no neighbor in it

how do you like your coffee

these days I think I will just drink tea

A Letter to My Grandfather

I have never told the whole truth when asked

why I feel the need to vote

why voting to me is of grave importance

I have not asked and don't know who to ask

I am aware my grandfather could not vote, never voted

did not have enough coins to pay the poll tax

or a pen to write answers to such a bizarre literacy test

missing one question in an impossible quiz of thirty

disqualifies you from voting, back then the struggle was real

unlike now when arguments ensue over rights

over religion, over why some believe their votes do not count

we live in a time we fight over two of the three colors

embedded in the American flag, fight merely because we have fist

fight over insignificant things, over situations

that are not situations, not struggles at all

I do not know exactly when it happened

when did we forget yesterday, last year

a middle passage later, tomorrow

one hundred years ago, a couple of bullets and a hanging since

when did we forget the last hashtag

last beating replayed on our view boxes

Steel Black

recorded in a police precinct because of melanin

how can we forget the last grand jury hearing

that was not so grand, when did we remember

we, we do not matter, we are begging

asking America to let us matter, asking for leniency

asking daily for a stay of execution

pleading for equal treatment

petitioning America to stop nationwide racial profiling

it should be illegal the way the police are constantly killing us

in our cars, at traffic stops, for a turn signal, red light

in our homes, on our front lawns, porches

at our grandmother's house, family business

I would ask my grandfather if he were here

if I could stand near the rock sitting on his chest

if I knew exactly how to remove two thousand pounds

of earth covering the box holding his bones

I would inquire, how did he grow old

how many friends did he lose, how old were they

how did he maneuver days when black was out of season

when no media outlet was there

to report when America came for you

when every black person could tell precautionary tales

of persecution, of illegal search and seizure

when there were no cameras explaining it was not our fault

we got stopped, frisked, shook down, accosted

how did he maintain his composure

when the color black had physical boundaries

there were places you were not allowed to venture

when railroad tracks were the most familiar landmark

used as a means of locating our townships

grandfather I bear your moniker, maybe even your likeness

you never realize the importance of memories until

you discover yours missing, until you have no memories

you label important, wish I knew your favorite song

which dances you enjoyed, how you sway the words you used

I have no tales to tell, no stories of old, no good just bad

Dear grandfather, oh how I need a word from you

to pass to seeds wondering why I never speak your name

how grand it would be if I could say you raised your daughter

and not abandoned her to fend for herself

if time were a mirror who knew every reflection

would be blurred, out of focus, the mirror would be no sided

who knew hindsight could really be blind

I pass them stories of their grandmothers

but not one word of the thoughts or dreams

from either one of their grandfathers

Steel Black

I can only wonder the lessons I would have learned

your absence leaves holes in my days, gaps in my ability to father

but oh how honored I am I am able to create

a legacy wearing your name it remains an American tragedy

I ashamed to inform you

I know, and I am sure you knew

black men have been missing for more than a century

been missing since they made milk cartons

since they have been able to send out amber alerts

since they were permitted to place pictures

on the walls of the post office, you would never know

what difference a grandfather makes in the lives of his seeds

there is something special about the way grandchildren

run their fingers through blessed gray locs

through a beard touched by time, Dear Grandfather

I wish you were here, or a poet, or a writer

wish I knew why you left - I would listen

wish I knew how you felt - I would care, wish I knew

what you thought, those are the diamonds

I would share with my grandchildren proudly

I wish you would have left a legacy of thought

It would be my pleasure to keep your words

growing, in our hearts and our memories

Black Girl

been told black man ain't posed to write

no black girl poem

ain't posed to know them troubles

that followed them from way back

ever since massah saw that ass naked

on them auction blocks

white men been chasing that black girl magic

been taking it without permission

been stealing black girls since

they made cars with cranks in the front

every black man knows how troubles

been following black girls

since they birthed, since they learned to walk

since they been black

they been black since Africa

since civilization got here

God should have created black girls first

maybe then this world wouldn't be so cruel

so angry at black men

so jealous of that black girl magic they born with

black men been knowing

Not Just Alphabets

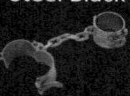

Steel Black

he posed to be protecting black girls

some of them had bad learning

thanking they god, thanking black girls

posed to do what they say

just cause they hands bigger

he ain't posed to used them as weapons

they bigger cause God knowed

how this shit was gone go down

how they gone steal us

how they gone separate us when we arrive

how to they gone take our clothes

make us stand bare ass naked

knew they gone chain us together

place us on them blocks

put us up for sale like cattle, like property

like we ain't really people or persons

temptation was in the plan

he even knew they hearts was black

can't control they self

when black beauty is sitting there ain't his

don't belong to nobody

black girls ain't posed to belong to nobody

why you think they got that magic

they should be able to pick who they give it to

ain't no black man posed

to write no black girl poem

ain't posed to know them troubles

that followed them from way back

black men posed to be protectors

that is why they hands bigger

why them shoulders a little wider

why they got bigger feet

posed to use that body to stand in front

them hands to move troubles aside

ain't no black girl got time for troubles

how she gone build all that magic

God blessed her with

if she gotta deal with troubles by herself

I've been told ain't no black man

posed to write no black girl poem

she got that magic all by herself

ain't gotta share it if she don't want to

let's just protect them, stop all this complaining

cause God is the one

give black girls all that magic

not us

Steel Black

Broken

I have been broken so many times

some mornings I break myself

into as many portions as possible

to see if I have gained new skills

of rebuilding me with everything

I thought for sure I was made of

some days needed parts are unable to fit

in the space they came from

discolored, misremembered, displaced

scattered emotions cannot be replaced

with new, transfigured, bartered or borrowed ones

no matter how many ways you try and make them fit

once I placed my right hand on my left arm

that day all my thoughts were written in reverse

some days I write in reverse

attempting to trace thoughts back to their origin

needing to know where broken comes from

initially I believed heaven sent me broken parts

for practice - to teach me to be an emotion mechanic

we must learn to repair ourselves

our hands are ours they have always been

it is our duty to master the use of fingers

to learn the purpose of thumbs

I know why the simultaneous movement of fingers

forms a closed fist - why knuckles are pointed

why wrist have eight small bones and two large ones

why they break so easily

why hands and fist are not weapons you can depend on

after reviewing my most embarrassing moments

I am no longer shy or embarrassed

when flaws reveal themselves

to unknowns who seek perfection

no matter how hard you work

to become a master at anything

it will only make you better not perfect

I was born with the anger my forefathers

arrived with, coupled with pain and tragedy

trapped in my double helix

I have learned not to depend

on any of America's story's being facts

we must consider them mere tales of reference

written by notable writers embellished

with the precision of a trained swindler

for the purpose of making great

Steel Black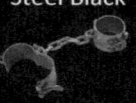

a country built by the hands of slave labor

the only great here is that we are great here

we have been great here for centuries

when asked of our native tongue

who knew tongues could be native

who knew tongues could be

anything other than stolen

there are excuses we will never use

explanations we will never hear

of where the trillions of dollars

plantation owners transferred from

slave labor to their kin was washed

clean of blood, closeted the skeletons

removed bones and ropes

to make present day currency just cash

we were brought here because hard work

is not for the faint of heart

none of our ancestors were faint of heart

we have arrived at the crossroads

where broken meets severed

I spent my life practicing broken

so I would know how it looked

when we arrived at this day

this point in history where backward

is not an option

where feet won't run, won't stop

will march, no matter how tired

how repetitive these actions may seem

feet won't quit - got a host of angels named

Wheatley, Angelou, Morrison, Butler

Hurston, Walker, McMillan, Lewis, Hughes

Baldwin, Baraka, Haley, Wright

not demanding we get it right

but honored we won't quit

how can we stop when free

free is right there - on that corner

broken - severed, ripped to shreds

I must believe heaven sent me broken parts

for practice - to teach me to be a culture mechanic

we must stop this war on color this black on black

this brother on brother - sister on sister

it is up to us to rebuild our self-esteem

how to walk, chest out, head up

back straight, left right left right

we must learn to repair ourselves

our hands are ours they have always been

Not Just Alphabets

Steel Black

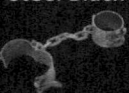

it is our duty to master the use of fingers

to know broken is not by mistake

we were snapped in two on purpose

by the history they forced us to survive

we are whole and here

we have been great for centuries

we were brought here because hard work

is not for the faint of heart

none of our ancestors were faint of heart

they are proud we keep this fight forward

they will not let our feet stop marching

know this for sure we will never be

faint of heart

Amen

on August 24, 1814, the British troops

attempted to turn the white house black

as if they knew in advance one day the occupant

would be the color of burnt wood after fire

it is amazing what intrinsic racism will do

to make sure the memory of those days

could not be traced by actions

everything constructed by executive orders

even the garden built by a black first lady

purposely removed, overwritten and demolished

what does the church say when the choir can't sing

when the pulpit is empty, when Covid hushed the sermons

in its temple, synagogue, mosque, religious centers

what does the church say when

there are no Amen or hallelujahs

in the mouths of parishioners

bouncing off the walls of its sanctuary

when boarded-up windows fail to tell night from day

when unmarked soldiers clear a path

to an abandoned structure once used

for worship just for you to escape the boredom

Steel Black

of the skeleton crewed white house

what amusement do you get from flash bangs

tear gas, rubber bullets, forcing

huddled masses scurrying to escape

when there can be no peace in protest

no good people on both sides

no questions why, why these actions

are still necessary after hundreds of years

of protest, of marching, of fighting for equality

for justice, for unequal ledgers to be balanced

what is the difference between a confederate general

made of stone holding a sword aimed toward heaven

or a commander and chief standing in front of a hollowed-out

place of worship holding a bible aimed toward heaven

there is no difference

they are both used as proof to the people

a lie can be the truth, a hero is

whatever they claim a hero to be

we are still here peaceful, marching, protesting

asking the almighty to take just us

use it to correctly spell justice

what does the church say

when racist claim they are not racist

when an administration cannot say black lives matter

when there are no good people on both sides

when justice refuse to remove her mask

so we can see her face and balance these scales

we have been stranded on since they

removed our chains, unshackled ankles

told us in scriptures our skin was the color of servitude

of bondage, of less than, not equal to

what does the church say when the choir can't sing

when the pulpit is empty

when Covid hushed the sermons

when there are no Amen or hallelujahs

bouncing off the walls of its sanctuary

when boarded-up windows

fail to tell innocence from guilty

fail to hold police accountable for their actions

when shots fired equal leave with pay

when they strive to make guilty the victim they accosted

when truth ain't truth and a hero

is whatever they claim a hero to be

what does the church say when God quit listening

when heaven closed its ears when all the angels

tucked wings and turned their backs

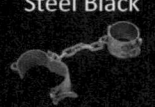# Steel Black

when glory is just greens

when praise can't be praise

when pride turns into a tourniquet

when you cannot tell protecting from attacking

when we know God is not the spirit of fear

all they want to do is make us fear

what does the church say

when the choir can't sing

when the hymnals are forgotten

when the worshipers are missing

when there is no more amazing grace

or swing low's coming forth to carry us home

what does the church say

when there are no more Amen or hallelujahs

from people learning to pray to stay alive

how do you say Amen when they keep killing us

like a sermon, like its Sunday

like turn that other cheek

like the holy in sabbath is a reference to bullets

as if they didn't rebuild the white house

after the fire

they call it the white in hopes its occupants

would always be the color of its paint

what does the church say

at the next black funeral

next press conference

next chest with death on the front

when the choir can't sing

when ain't no praises to sing about

when ain't no more hallelujahs

and we used our last Amen

at the last internment service

and the police are still on vacation

do we still say Amen

Steel Black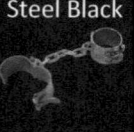

Better Self

do you ever stop and listen to yourself?

speaking of unity but only forgiving

those who do not look like you

we say we love one another

as we pick and choose who to love

excluding those we are unwilling to talk to

making finding a resolution impossible

who would believe an argument

of words over words could break a community

some of the issues are so small

they shouldn't be issues at all

we scream black lives matter

while the number of blacks killed by blacks

can't be found in true statistics

I've wondered how anyone can find anger

when you ask for truth

and it doesn't sound as the song

you thought should be sung

of your greatness

we all want to be great

but we struggle to survive

where is the greatness in that

I wish everything I write

didn't frighten the reader

don't want you to feel the slave in me

has control of my pen

I could have written most of these poems

four hundred years ago using the same lines

I want to build with you something glorious

but every day we are struggling to survive

how can that be glorious

we build fences instead of planting fields

can't keep giving these youth

a plan of action we refuse to follow

asking them to look past their differences

as they watch us build clicks because of ours

wish we could use outside eyes to see ourselves

record our actions as others record our actions

I would hope like me you would be ashamed

I've been silent for so long

knew you couldn't hear me

complaining without resolve seems so futile

our first amendments rights has been revoked

no one wants to hear your opinion

if it doesn't sound like theirs

if you have a mind of your own

you must remain on your own

I am often curious

Steel Black

do you ever listen to yourself

wonder how your opinion grew in concrete

how anchored in your truth your feet rest

how your lips move in sync

only with those singing just like you

I would hope like me you are ashamed

to claim you are a scribe

to call yourself a carver of truth

to grip pens as a poet is supposed to

stealing verses not verifying ownership

I would hope we are striving to be better

to do more than visit stages

put your life behind the mic

then listen to the music

we all need to stop and listen to ourselves

check our verses against our days

see which one means more

I pray we find forgiveness

it is never for the person

you think you are forgiving

we can't find truth or get better

without forgiving ourselves first

there is greatness in that

I believe we all have a bit of greatness

residing in our better self

Centuries of Misunderstanding

there are dates of the first ships arriving

off the coast of places we will not mention

we won't agree anyway

it has been that way for centuries

we haven't spoken the same language

since our tongue was stolen

the distance between cotton field and kitchen

makes our words too whispered

too broken English to sound familiar

all these years later

we still love like runaway slaves

trying to find each other on foreign soil

the time from captive to free

can be measured in minutes or days

time refuses to let go of such tragic beginnings

even now we suffer the same fate

confederate militia or city police

treat us as if we are not supposed to be

beyond the perimeters of where they tell us

chains are too familiar to be forgotten

some educators attempted to change

Steel Black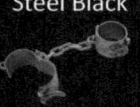

slaves to immigrants thinking one word

would make history easier to swallow

thinking we would not notice

centuries drowned in sentences

we will not let you create a way out

you have benefited from everything we have created

patents, labor, the strength of black women

feeding and teaching your children to be better

your conscious must suffer for acts neither you nor I

can find the heart to forgive or forget

I can hear the train coming, see the waves of regret

you look like those before you who look like those before them

same speech, same racist, same hate, same color

you bear the pains passed through your blood

so much privilege coursing through your veins

I've seen the red line you drew in the sand

on the other side of the tracks

you hoped our community would not survive the storms

thought pissing in the wind would make you god

there are no saviors here, no angels, no feathers

in any of the wings we have left

no banks or stores, no businesses we can invest in

we have been taught to fear investing in anyone

who looks like us or ourselves

we recognize the culture of hate

as if hate was a part of our culture

how can we build a family or village

when all we have known is destruction

you have diluted our linage

with the rape of our fore mothers

we are both black and white less white than black

one drop of melanin equals no privilege

even our DNA has strands missing

we believe everything you say when every word

you have shared for years were lies all your stories falsehoods

you could not spit the truth if you drank it by the keg

here we are walking backwards through time

still struggling, still marching

it is not just Selma, Mississippi, Alabama

the south mentality moved north while we were sleeping

how can we explain the unexplainable

schools are centers for miseducation

plantations are corporate sponsored prisons

hangings are choke holds, knees on necks,

bullets in backs, in fronts, in apartments, in houses

on corners, in Walmarts, in parking lots

Steel Black

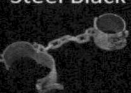

bullets are what they use to quail the spirit of fear

black is bones wrapped in fear for skin

you you you you you you you

you thin thin thin think think think

you think I stutter - I don't

that is time catching up to

generations of black men

for years yelling the same shit

stop, don't hang me, don't shoot

can't breathe, hands up

echoes are the hardest thing to get right

as for me

I'm just trying to get it right

Distractions

a hummingbird, butterfly

a swartz sticker, firefly

a long gun unsafely on a rack

hanging in the back window

of any monster truck in the south

a trophy formed into statue

in remembrance of slavery

a general brandishing

a sword who lost the war

a confederate flag waving proudly

as if we still pick cotton

as if we ain't found the other two fifths

of ourselves they been hiding since when

any verbal reference to the great again

any monument or celebration

of the good ole days

are mere distractions

hoping we will not read the new subtractions

from the civil rights act

the provisions removed from the voting rights act

praying we will not notice

Steel Black

the number of polls

not opening this voting season

the tweets, the disgusting phrases

used to describe minority women

the lies shared while men who pleaded guilty

are pardoned by the same person they went to jail for

the beats hiding the words in that song you like

the shades worn by any of our women at midnight

the beautiful scarf around her neck

in the blistering August sun

child support filed immediately after graduation

when you cannot tell the difference

between cannot find and kidnapped

there is a host of things we let

distract us from our purpose

from the goals we told ourselves

were ours to attain, it is impossible

to retrieve moments lost or spent idle

we have more power than we think

more focus than we have yet to use

do not let the unnecessary distract you

from the goals right at your fingertips

Family

I carved another poem today

tore it from my left ventricle

or maybe my left arm

this body is filled with thoughts

needing to be verbalized

do not even bleed anymore

it does not hurt as much

I am getting used to the pain

never experienced childbirth

but this one could have formed

in my stomach nine months ago

in no way am I claiming

to be the origin of life or verses

mothers cannot be replaced with words

I know the birth of a nation

can be found in how we treat the gifts

we were blessed to receive

this is just the tip of the mountain

can't be considered the top

until we build a formidable base

imagine we are dust particles

Steel Black

waiting to unite

we were once chained

Interlocked, not of our own doing

there was a time before now we understood

discovered common ground

we were once bound to one another love first

considered everyone who looked like us family

didn't place a grade on economics

we've forgotten the strength we have together

the power we had in unity

attachments earned while fighting the same fight

got me hoping if I shake you hard enough

if I can keep your eyes focused

for more than three minutes

you would notice black on black

is more than a crime scene

more than these wagons circled

surrounded by a posse of police

we are better than the gangsters

and cowboys we tell ourselves we are

the swinging saloon doors

at the entrance of the titty bar

cannot be the only place we meet

this stage is more than the launch pad

you plan to use to rocket your career

into the atmosphere

imagine we were all angels

before we woke up

someone stole our wings

lied to our faces

documented the tale in history books

told us we were less than human

we listened and read it enough times

now it's the religious doctrine we pray by

teach our children the words to

no matter how wide we open our eyes

we can't see ourselves the same

if we came from dirt

imagine we are dust particles

waiting to unite

we could form a mountain of us

complete with all of our broken

and begin to become whole again

I carved another poem today

it didn't hurt as much as the others

but I have a gift to offer you

Steel Black

got a handful of yesterday's

I need you to examine

somewhere in their passing

we should be able to see ourselves whole

revisit the strength shared when we knew unity

when we knew this melanin made us family

before the lies - before you believed

we are less than human, we can fix this - fix us

mountains are mere particles of dust

that completely understood had unbreakable faith

in the concept and power of unity

I will stand here - scream these words

shake you until you wake up

we are mountains

that's better than being angels

there are no requirement of wings

to build ourselves whole again

to force our life to remember

we are stone masons carvers of commandments

original man, empires destroyed

we can be whole again dust and wings forming mountains

united we are family, please believe me

we have always been family

The Devil's Hand

I've purposely neglected

and climbed over all the bones

in my closet to get here

most Monday's I grip my pen

as a shot gun with a hair trigger

or the switch on the electric chair

thinking no good can come from this

my relationship with pens is what lead me to fire

a pyromaniac holding a pension for burning pages

paper burns quick so you have to write fast

who's to say for sure pens are not people

and cannot write themselves whole

a palm filled with ink is considered the devil's hand

since poets are bearers of truth

no one in the country we hold dear

could hold any more truth than we already have

in America no matter how brown my skin appears

I am black as black can be

I am miseducated black, relocated black

no medical insurance black, lost culture black

don't know where I come from black

Steel Black

there is no record to the fifth card

in a dead man's hand

the day Wild Bill Hickock was assassinated

2 aces black 2 eights black

no reference to red or white

the remaining card held no significance

when it comes to assassinations

incarcerations and death, in our America

it is always and will always be black

midday black, midnight black, Monday morning black

black Friday black, black thought black

prison industrial complex black

I've been picking pieces apart with the devil's hands

since I was taught to hold fire

ashes and hurt inside my pen

I write with the conviction

of a condemned serial poet

didn't ask for this job, did not apply

was not chosen, don't know how it came about

sometimes it is your duty to assume responsibility

until help gets here, no one has declared

help is on its way

we have but three choices

shut up, march or fight

the first we can no longer abide by the premise

for silence makes you culpable of the same crime

you turned a blind eye to not witness

you would believe most of the police

have a Master of Fine Arts Degree

from the same Arian University as the Grand Wizard

while we attended The Peace Academy

without earning a degree

it doesn't make sense

they shoot us - we march, they hang us - we march

they choke us with knees - we march

they strangle us with hands - we march

they arrest us without cause - we march

the only common denominator for the last century

in every act of aggression and pain

America inflicted on us is... we march

I've been picking pieces apart with the devil's hands

each finger pointing to an African nation

as if we were chosen to be part of this

diabolical experiment created by the devil himself

how long can a people last

when you have taken their last

Not Just Alphabets

Steel Black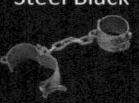

bit of hope, son, daughter, last prayer

last breath, last ounce of faith

here we are still standing on our last leg

I've heard heaven helps those who helps themselves

we will not ask for permission or approval

will not raise our hands or stand in line

will not wait to be added as five fifths

to a document you never wanted

or approved

our skin to be a part of

I write not because I have to

God has given me no other option

we have arrived at this point

because we have no other option

I have been picking pieces apart

with the devil's hands

you will soon see, when those same five fingers

that chose us chooses you

you will realize there is no place to hide

no route, no refuge, no escape

no blessed reassurances, no grace sufficient

you will realize just as we did

you will have no other option

Harriett's Feet

America has a way of blackening our thoughts

rewriting wrongs right, changing history's left eye

right in front of us, demanding we do not see what

we witnessed firsthand, how dare I let another February

come and go without writing woman back into her bones

I refuse to let another day go by without revealing

the great stolen from her legacy, Nike ing or rather Tubman ing

the goatness of her feet, if any person deserve a shoe

made in their honor her profile would fit G.O.A.T. perfectly

I guess no one knew before she showed us the distance

between slavery and heaven is only 800 miles, ergo the song

when I get to heaven gonna stomp all over Gods heaven

heaven, everybody talking bout heaven ain't going there

heaven, maybe no one knew heaven and free

bore the same address, you could not find it by yourself

Harriet is the sole reason we now have a GPS with us

at all times, in the slightest instance a new Moses arrives

knowing where freedom resides they will be able to track

our movement, it is easy to get lost without a guide

imagine a woman with a voice possessing angelic properties

whispering in the dark was loud enough for followers

Steel Black

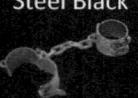

to know which direction to move, how fast or slow

America has yet to find all sixteen routes Harriett created

from bondage to freedom, she left no footprints

and no one who followed her shared details

of safe houses or landmarks, I have no idea how

it is done with such consistency , why it is commonplace

to subtract humanity from black women

before history writes their names

list their amazing accomplishments, maybe it is the

poet's duty to write them whole, America will scream

whatever negatives possible to darken their light

we be charcoal moons, black suns, white teeth

glistening in black holes, we are a forever

burning flame in this unquenchable terror

of a story, history has penned us flawed, simple minded

imperfect, this is the why we look for bad in us

before we are able to see good, we've been broken

on purpose, America taught us well, we have whitelisted

ourselves, sacrificed our dark skin, given our names

for the cause, they will Carver your peanuts and Peter Pan

or Jiffy your peanut butter, you cannot see how they Hanes

and Fruit of the Loomed your cotton but stole Sam's last name

for years top designers been trying to steal her feet

where do you think the idea for red bottoms came from

we still search for reasons so many preferred

to remain captive, stay slave, maybe massah

only beat them or raped their wives on Thursdays

maybe massah wasn't as horrible as history paints

no one spoke of the distance could it be instead of miles

heaven was measured for them in time, in steps

in casualties or hiding places, once they heard how long

it took to get to free many were discouraged

became complacent, imagine having your free

and willing to give it up each time you went back

each time you received a letter, a calling

a message more are ready to make it to heaven

if America would have storied Harriet woman

made her flesh and dwelt amongst us

spoke her monthly as no consequence

she did not Clairol or Maybelline, did not wear

eye shadow or lipstick, if America wrote her

feminine in the context of great

it would not have taken as long,

Harriet would have earned women the right

to vote, would have proven women could run nations

could be president, I must believe every person

Steel Black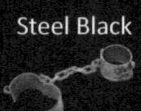

Harriet led from captive to free immediately

begin praying for her shoes as if the souls

of the newly free could gather enough heaven

to form extra ordinary soles to protect her feet

Harriet must be the only person granted by the most high

replacement parts, how many miles on expired feet

do you think she traveled, maybe she was granted

new soles because of the souls she saved

have you ever walked so far you forgot

what far was or used to be, America shares a hate

hate relationship with anyone, especially a black woman

with a reputation larger than any writer of historically

empirical information allows her to have

they took her humanity, wrote her less than human

removed her femininity did not speak or write her

as female, I refuse to let another day go by

without revealing the stolen from her legacy

the black in her woman, the heaven in her bones

the God in her feet, I thank heaven for her feet

Dear Covid 19

dear democratic hoax,

Chinese pandemic, corona virus,

Covid-19, 45 I take no responsibility

can't test everyone don't need to know

how many are truly infected

let the cruise ship stay at sea

can't let the numbers go up

our commander and chief said

you are merely a shallow pond

that could never come ashore

a spec of dust searching for a sandstorm

a breeze that will subside at the first light of day

here we are...

a small island off the coast of New York

freezers, refrigerator trucks and ditches

for burial sites for those unclaimed

hospitals overwhelmed with no room in the inns

military tents temporary beds for emergencies

box cars filled with body bags

minorities are the majority in lock up

prisons are incubators - hubs for black death

Steel Black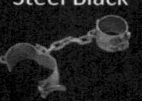

the coldest winter in Nevada

was when covid 19 arrived in spring

this is the second time since 2005

we are left with lies – the first were

thousands abandoned on rooftops

Corona and Katrina must be the best of kin

there are still those listening

to an administration

who won't wear mask

claim the numbers are false

unprepared for a battle of this magnitude

unlike the black death, Spanish Flu

blankets full of surprises

the innumerable diseases

Christopher carried to the islands

we fit the covid as if it were

designed for justice

I mean just us

like the putrid belly of hollowed out ships

the prison plantation industrial complex

the stock market was built of us for them

we were the original meat to be traded

in Texas, a recaptured black man

was worth his weight in acres

we will always be America's

top money makers

this population must be lowered

because of global warming

imagine a disease that can attach itself

perfectly to melanin

priceless

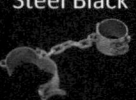

Steel Black

The Negro Can Dance

you don't know jealousy

don't know how joy feels

when it comes in the morning

how glory is a song

you never heard until you sing it

happy are dance steps you are taught in your sleep

some mornings the ancestors will wake you

feet moving to rhythms only they know

to a song they sang in the dusk and darkness

history tells us how hard work

that sunup to sundown thing

leaves you with no time left in your day

for anything but food and rest

my ancestors whispered in my ears

took my hand showed me as I slumbered

how they snuck out far from the shanty huts

far past the first line of trees

how they made a small fire

just large enough for the warmth

to reach out and touch them

until moving created warmth in they bones

how massah would sneak out

when he heard the melodies

hide in the brush and try to feet dance

as he watched them move

pain can't go nowhere unless

you throw some happy with it

we should have learned over time

all this hurt America tosses our way

can't stop our glory

can't force our feet to stop moving

even back then them whites knowed

the negro can dance

the negro can play instruments they never seen

fix that hair like goddesses and angels

cook great dishes they never tasted

even massah knowed the negro can dance

why you think he hid in that brush

every time he heard the melodies

every time he saw the glow of flames

of them fires they danced around

even massah knowed the negro can dance

even America knows these negroes can dance

been knowing it for centuries

Steel Black

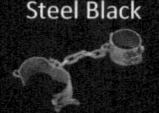

built schools trying to steal our feet

the only reason video was created

was so massah didn't have to hide

in that brush no mo when he saw the flames

when the fire started

when he traced the sound and melodies

through the dusk and darkness

past that first line of trees

massah want to learn to feet dance too

and believe me

America has known for centuries

got video, kept books, silent movies

them hand drawn sketches

and vinyl records as proof

artist traced the movement of they feet

where do you think that two step

and cotton eyed joe came from

America has known for centuries

the negro can dance

Fingers Never Stop Talking

I wish I never learned sign language

I mean the language of listening

sound, I mean poetry

I wish I did not know the power of words

written as sacrifice, verses ripped away

for the sake of remembering

of releasing, of painting history truthfully

I wish my hands had five pens instead of fingers

I keep finding lost pieces of me

trapped in syringes I prefer to label writing utensils

my fingers will often forget what I tell them

they will write what they wish,

scribe what they've been told

what they know must be shared

ears are not ears, they are hinges

for hanging portraits

lips are not lips, these are sound guards

to shield you from projectiles

able to pierce locked emotions

this mouth is not a mouth it is a picture frame

I prefer to paint in sound

Not Just Alphabets

Steel Black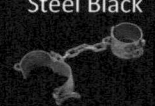

my voice is a collection

of my mother's love heavily seasoned

with my father's pain

the pages I carve my life in

are made of muddy water

footprints gathered from every ocean floor

our forefathers and foremothers

made their final resting place

we all must participate in this uncovering

we keep finding new portions of us

lost in ledgers, secret documents

covered by secret documents

hidden in books with titles

we did not know existed

truth is not easy when the burden

of remembering is passed on through

the language of death

death is a language, why do you think

it is so hard for fathers to speak

when police murder their unarmed sons

black mothers has been the calming voice

in America from the moment she held

and hushed the wailing

of little white babies on plantations

fed them from breast her own offspring

would never taste

somedays I wish my fingers would stop this pain

stop telling these truths America keep hiding

in news conferences, in presidential executive orders

in bulletins and special reports

I can't say for sure if this breathing

I am allowed to do Is fuel

for these fingers to never stop talking

this is not my purpose - it is ours

these are not my words - it is a song

it is a twentieth century hymn

I was given these gifts these passages

have been passed down from generations

of black men who could not be themselves

could not write, were not allowed

to be properly educated

could not speak freely without consequence

could not walk through front doors

sit at lunch counters

could not vote without a poll tax

these are the separate and unequals

Steel Black

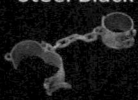

no longer up for debate or discussion

parts of this America

we will not sing or hum about

one day I will ask these fingers

can I just tell my part

there will come a time

every part will be shared

every story will matter

every life will have purpose

but this right now ain't mine

this is the first time I can say

unity is a possibility

we must fill page after page

with dreams of the dreamless

tell the stories before now

could not see the light of day

these fingers are not just fingers

they are the landing strip

for centuries of screams and atrocities

giving voice to the voiceless

most will not realize the struggle of truthing

until you complete the greatest task

you were petitioned by heaven to write

heaven did not give you this gift

because you deserved it

did not give it to you for your benefit or glory

the task of scribe was burden to many before you

these pages of sacrifice, these psalms are necessary

ask no questions, for this - this be God's work

this is how heaven sends an S O S

these are the psalms the angels wish they could write

I will keep filling empty pages with hopes and wishes

most of these truths will be mistaken for a poem

some may sing as a hymn, read as a prayer

either way, I am sending them to heaven

just in case they turn out to be both

Steel Black

Lesson on Marches

throughout our history I cannot recall marching

without watchers, overseers, tiki torches, militia

police, FBI, armed guards, out of uniform Klansmen

firemen hoses at the ready, trained attack dogs

billy clubs drawn, marksmen on roof tops

handguns cocked and loaded, notifying the national guard

without each step monitored, without a signed

pre stamped no march order by a statesman

police chief, governor, president, demanding our feet

stay within the bounds of our shoes, our legs

not take us past main street, past the doubled

white line on the bridge to the capital, demanding

our feet could not move ten feet toward

whatever direction we were told would lead us to free

there was always a street, building, sidewalk, marked

too far for a black body to stand, there are places we

could not live, would refuse us applications, streets

we could not walk or drive, could not look at, visit

on January 6, 2021 I cannot believe the things

my eyes witnessed, recorded on video by news anchors

men and women, maybe I am just one eyewitness

to a lesson on marches, documented visual proof

flags will not be accosted as long as you hold them

high enough to be seen in the distance, as long as you

make dixie swing in the wind as if it be tree

I watched a cluster of flags form keys to locked doors

at the capital where attending officers stepped aside

as if ordered by a higher authority, I learned in an instant

this is how American citizens are treated whose skin

do not resemble night, citizens never listed as three fifths

who do not need added amendments to grant them American

do not need their right to vote ratified, who will never ask

if it is alright this year if they matter, will never look like

someone else even if they are the one on the wanted poster

maybe if we confederated our red, black and green

militia ed our skin, hummed 'wish I was in dixie'

under the whispered chant of black lives matter

what could make us matter, maybe if we joined the shriek

all lives matter, yesterday in total amazement the difference

between white and wishful thinking clearly visible

as we watched privileged men and women move

with reckless abandonment, laughing as they destroyed

property, media equipment, push and shove police with no recourse

watched as most of them carried weapons, took selfies with

Steel Black

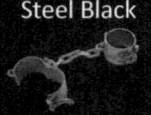

friendlies in uniform, some were

ushered by capital police

into prohibited space, usually weapons

not allowed, I sat remembering Ferguson

Dallas, New York, Wisconsin

Kentucky, Chicago, California, Georgia

Oklahoma, Washington and every other state

where armored vehicles were used

police shields held high, weapons drawn

Kicking, beating dark skin citizens

arresting peaceful protesters

for marching to city hall, capital hill

the governor's mansion, standing in the park

marching down any street in America

where an unarmed minority person was slain

the killers puts on their uniform everyday

ninety eight percent of the murders are still free

yesterday - we received a lesson on marches

I guess it really matters what color your skin

how big your flag and which

symbolic emblem rests in its center

A Little Note

after re reading the constitution

I really need to see the original document

the one kept behind glass, lock and key

what if there are hand written notes

on the back, concise messages left just for us

I do not believe they thought it would take

this long for former slaves to overcome

the obstacles purposely placed in our path

they knew reading was fundamental

didn't think we were fun or had the capacity

to comprehend anything beyond the information

given us they believed useful

maybe one of the messages would read

"we tried to include you, but no one knows

how much this free will be worth in the future

we cannot give you a hand up or hand out

while using ours to keep you down at the moment

we don't have any hands that are free"

I can see Jefferson's pen moving, I imagine it would read

"none of us really wanted to own slaves,

we were not really into running plantations

Steel Black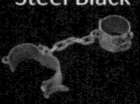

beating or having concubines

it was the in thing, like Jordan's, Gucci

Versace, Fendi, Skims it was always trending

the only ones who didn't own slaves

were slaves, we wrote it that way

to make sure they could not own themselves"

maybe if I reread the Preamble

it would make clear there is no we

in we the people, that tranquility part

I understand now, they knew back then

we wouldn't go along with all the plans they had

to take back whatever progress we made

wherever we lived would be disenfranchised

the neighborhood gentrified, converted

and overpriced, don't know how they foresaw

if they did not keep their promises

there could be trouble ahead

good trouble, trouble requiring police

to have no moral values when approaching anyone black

trouble in the fifties and sixties

lunch counter trouble, marching trouble

speech trouble, white only bathrooms trouble

good troubles where tear gas

dogs, beatings and bullets

will be needed to break up peaceful protest

good trouble like a seventeen-year old

with a long gun protecting property

that ain't his trouble

good trouble like the stock market

reaching the highest it has ever been

without investments by former slaves

the people on which the stock market was built

good trouble like an administration refusing

to abide by the words in the civil rights act

the removal and interference of rights of

minority voters written on the same document

they will not let me see, all those amendments added

stuck for a while, I guess over time they began to fall off

what if there were notes attached to the back

of the constitution or declaration of independence

that didn't stick, back then post it wasn't a company

didn't know they would be needed until now

I need to see the original document

see where sixteen more signatures

could fit, men refusing to agree

men unwilling to sign a document

Steel Black

that didn't have a bill of rights

they wanted removal of the protections

for the continuation of slavery and the slave trade

George Mason could have penned a secret

on the back of one of those documents

a little note explaining not everyone wanted

this nation to be built on the color of one's skin

I imagine he would have penned

"we cannot hold these trues to be self-evident

about all men, if everything we say is not true"

imagine the impact of knowing

in 1787 some men were on our side

wanted the representation in congress to be equal

thought three fifths made no sense

what parts of a human must be removed

to make them a fraction of a person

if there are notes on any of the documents

we need to locate them soon

ink on parchment is said to last a little over

one hundred years, it is time we find them

or write new notes for those who will search

the same documents after we are gone

Essay

The Inhumanity Clause

The Inhumanity Clause

It is not hard to fathom the possibility of alternate clauses appearing within historical documents newly found under the scrutiny of Google and Wikipedia. These days you can ask questions pertaining to any subject in the comfort of your home or business and get an answer. Often, the response will be something neither of us expected to hear. Yes hear, each one has a distinctive voice, Alexa, Siri, Soundform, Facebook Portal, Amazon Echo and a host of other interactive virtual assistants. Each can assist you in your quest for knowledge. Most Americans are aware the Three Fifths Clause in the constitution, increased the representation in government by southern states but did not offer any resolve or resolution to the slaves themselves. Neither of these points are up for discussion they are facts and cannot be changed even if we wanted to change them. We are here to discuss the possibility of America having hidden in one of her historical documents an 'Inhumanity Clause'.

It is not farfetched for a country with no moral compass or empathy for the citizens they deem unworthy of participation in its freedoms or inalienable rights, to have hidden clauses in secret documents. We must imagine how much thought, group debate and objective deliberation had to be considered before completely omitting an entire group of citizens from its original charter declaring independence. No matter what is done on the outside, they expect full participation in the great American song.

You are supposed to sing with right hand across your heart including the third verse, although it will never be sung out loud. Just for the record, the third verse of the Star-Spangled Banner written by Francis Scott Key reads:

"And where is that band who so vauntingly swore, That the havoc of war and the battle's confusion A home and a Country should leave us no more? Their blood has wash'd out their foul footstep's pollution. No refuge could save the hireling and slave From the terror of flight or the gloom of the grave, And the star-spangled banner in triumph doth wave O'er the land of the free and the home of the brave."

Should it not be inhumane if the country you fought, shed blood, went to war for wants you to harmonize a song about your own demise? There is so much animosity, anger and hostility toward any non-Caucasian citizen who questions the meaning of the words in this verse. As if the meaning is not clear enough in the writing and reading of the words. You are considered un-American if you do not sing "No refuge could save the hireling and slave, From the terror of flight or the gloom of the grave". It just so happens each time the song is sung they stick closely to the first verse for safety.

How does it work? How am I to smile with right hand over my heart and sing? For so many years we mimicked motions and movements as demanded. We moved our lips even if we did not know the words. We marched to cadences that were off beat merely because we were told to march. Not now, not here, I refuse to blindly go in the direction unattached hands point anymore. I will not sing a song of my demise. I am searching because there must be a secret document, a legitimate reason none of the officers who shoot and kill unarmed black men and women are not being held accountable. It must be considered inhumane that any black citizen can be taken to court and charged using video footage as evidence, but no matter how many cameras show the wrongdoing of police officers the evidence must be further evaluated. It must be inhumane how week after week unarmed black men are being shot, some in their backs while walking or running away. Most videos seen where an officer stops a black man usually ends with a trip not to the hospital, but to the morgue. You can search the internet and find multiple cases of white men, young and old baring weapons, not obeying orders yelled by police officers yet if arrested will have their day in court.

Imagine with me, what document could hold such a clause for all these years and none of us have discovered its whereabouts? Which amendment would you choose? The second with guns would be a good place to start. I believe America would change her laws instantly if fifty percent of the minorities in this country began to purchase firearms for the safety of their home or workplace. Imagine the horror if every black person of voting age purchased a weapon, a firearm during the same week or month. I must believe there would be new questions added to whatever application is necessary for gun ownership. Or maybe somewhere in the nineteenth amendment that gave the right to vote to women. You can use the women part loosely because black women did not appear to be a part of this great monumental occasion. I would consider it inhumane while the nation celebrates the end of women suffrage it is not completely true it is the end. Black women suffered another five or more generations before accomplishing the same feat, the right to vote.

Could be in 2013 as the Supreme Court rolled back provisions of the 1965 Voting Rights Act a clause such as this could find a home. It always seems we are the last to know when rights or privileges fought for, died for and won years ago are taken back. An Inhumanity Clause would find a perfect fit in the secret retrieval of advancements or rather setbacks we are facing under an administration that is proud to place us back in our proverbial place.

Let us address a frightening truth in the year twenty twenty. Out of more than one hundred and ninety-eight permanent judges appointed over the last three years, not one of them black. What percentage is that? How inhumane is this? Could it be an accident? Maybe the Inhumanity Clause is not in writing, is not printed on any document. Maybe it is in the actions of those voted in office that do not have the all of American citizens in their plans. We must consider it inhumane if laws are passed or actions taken treating any of the minorities in this country less than. If police are not held accountable for their actions when the result is death. If states, governors, attorney generals do not speak truthfully at press conferences when addressing the out right murder of citizens without provocation.

Maybe we do not need a clause, an amendment or new laws that use the language of inclusion. Maybe if America could abide by the laws we have presently and uphold truth and justice in the application of them. This is the best country in which to live without question. It is somewhere in the word equality we find fault in the system. We have never been an equal partner in the freedoms every privileged American holds dear. Somewhere in the writing of the foundation of American politics we were left out on purpose. We still struggle for the proper interpretation of the phrase "all men are created free". Shouldn't we be a part of the all men? If so, why are we still fighting to be equal?

The definition of Inhumane is:

in·hu·mane / ˌin(h)yo͞oˈmān/ adjective

without compassion for misery or suffering; cruel.

I Dream in Revolutions

there were monsters in my closet, under my bed

viewed in moments of closed eye conversations

I could see through the dense dark shadows

everything I thought I was afraid of

heard the revolution would come

maybe it would or would not be televised

sources vary per description

heard free was the battle we were not prepared to fight

did not know it was coming, were not given a proper description

I dream in revolutions, dream nowhere

within the borders of these 50 stolen bodies of dirt

was safe for dark skin men like me

how many presidents raped and pillaged black women

before an embarrassed America ruled it illegal

before this nation found a hoard of bastard children

they were not willing to claim - to name

I dream in revolutions – dreamed ink on old paper are just old lies

men wearing wigs ruling the new land were just crossdressers

penning names on constitutions

was only practice for perfect penmanship

we suffer from a host of diseases and afflictions

Steel Black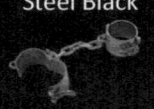

doctors have purposely misdiagnosed us for centuries

they hid us in fields of cotton, cane and tobacco

didn't want us to find ourselves

left many of our people too afraid to open up

lips sealed for generations, closets filled with luggage

stuffed with everything our grandparents

were too embarrassed to let loose

every illness mental or otherwise are listed

in the big black bible we kept on the coffee table

mental illness in our communities

are the biggest secrets our parents have been keeping

suicide and depression are words we kick like cans

down the proverbial by ways of our caged minds

can't whisper, can't let others know

how uncomfortable we've become with quiet

silence got too many words, too many syllables we can't spell

can't talk about where we go from here

or who's feet we use to get to there

got ghost trapped in walls, spirits floating through ceilings

bodies left in streets uncovered

these are not dreams, we should know the truth

America got problems with us marching

us wanting the things she promised

got problems keeping her word

to the indigenous people, to us

to every person making up this melting pot

got problems keeping her word even to herself

I dreamed there was a revolt every black in America

went out to vote we changed some shit that day

I dream in revolutions - dream that little black kids

would not have to go through all the shit

we have piled on the bottom of our shoes

repeating after echoes will not make you a mountain

no matter how loud you scream

mountains can't distinguish whats truth or lie

you would think its fireworks the way the kill us

nights when the full moon ain't that bright

sounds like celebrations, like the fourth of you lie

every trip to the store we pray

as loud as we can, driving slow lights on

as if we are in a funeral procession

home ain't never been no guarantee

I dreamed I spit a revolution to the top of mountains

to podcast, twitter, Instagram, YouTube, on Facebook

I dream in revolutions in high definition

ain't no room for tv if all you do is listen to the media

Steel Black

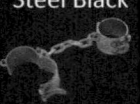

can't fit no records in that juke box of a brain

no play list when all we got is lists of names

of those slaughtered by police there were decisions

decided long before we knew how to listen

ears ain't clocks can't keep time can't feet dance

to drums when the only music is gunfire

for years we have all danced to the rhythm of triggers

got tap shoes made of badges and spent shells

streets so full of orange flares and caution tape

can't tell who calling my name from the afterlife

must be something important to share

I dream ghost want to explain to me what happened

making me take notes in these poems

God gives me to finger

I dreamed the revolution came and we were ready

had our good shoes on, covid mask, fist raised high

what if we didn't have to dream?

what if we voted just in case?

what if we stop hating and killing each other?

what would happen then?

would we even have to sleep?

would I still be dreaming in revolutions?

Dixie

when at every turn

you are surrounded by confederate flags

you will notice and remember each one

it is not something you can forget

no matter how hard you try not to remember

the first time I sat in court

in a small town in Mississippi

Andrew Jackson and confederate flag to my left

old glory embarrassed and leaning to my right

I knew before my case was heard

there would be no justice here today

each time I pass a house

porch swing and confederate flag

swaying to the same song

wishing they were still in Dixie

I can hear the argument

this is our history

we just want to remember

but how can you hold on to something

covered in injustice

bathed in hate, murder and slavery

Steel Black

I'm guessing if a policeman can accost

beat and arrest a young black female

charge her with accosting him

and resisting arrest while in pursuit

of a bald black man yielding a machete

blacks no longer have the right to gender

we will all always be guilty

before proven innocent

always fit the description

always identified as suspect

I hate to spoil the end of the story

but behind every 50 stars and old glory

there is a confederate flag lurking to be noticed

humming Dixie under the star mangled banner

we sing with hand over heart

making sure we are still breathing

it only takes one frown - red light – stop sign

left turn – traffic stop – peaceful protest

before any one of us can be rendered

chalk

I wish I was in Dixie hurray hurray

In Dixieland I had my plan

to live down south in Dixie

White Out

can't run, can't jog,

can't sit in your store

can't vote, can't drive

can't be black no more

saying black lives matter

makes your privilege sore

check your DNA

you're not white to the core

history is proof

you're just a copy cat

big lips, big ass

you weren't born like that

you spend most of your days

trying to be white black

trying to tan your skin

to be the right shade of black

Steel Black

Black Bodies, Black Bullets, Black Dreams

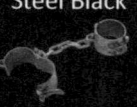

yesterday I was nearly eight miles from home

before the Sun turned on, before sunlight

caught me dragging this skin across the city

when is the last time Black was granted safe passage

even on your way to purpose down Destiny Lane

there are few choices you have when this skin is home

everything we need to accomplish must be performed in darkness

I keep checking to see if Black has an expiration date

stamped on it at birth , does it come with a warranty

are there replacement parts , are there safe words

to create safe travels for any of us in this country

it always seems death in our communities comes in both

black and white or is that black and blue

when death is by blue, we fight, we march, we burn, we are we

it is getting hard to not see black death by black hands

on black streets in black communities

what if they began to sell black bullets

a kind of heads-up which days would be the worst

we would be prepared to print new tee shirts

create new rest in peace slogans, new hashtags

I am sure Amazon and Google will find ways

to promote the sell of black bullets at discounted prices

black bullets would be perfect

at least we would know it is coming

know there will be no marches, no signs, only funerals

no protest for us killing us, no defunding the community

no money there anyway, no grand jury hearing

to suppress the truth, to edit the video footage

to give the shooter leave with pay

if you ask America and listen to the answer

you will discover Black Bodies has already been discounted

when it comes to the stock market and international trade

since its inception black has forever been listed as penny stock

in times like these we must wonder are there still Black Dreams

no hope, no stimulus, no work, no dollars

no food, no testing for this Covid

as our communities suffer at a higher rate than most

we are left wondering are there still Black Dreams

can they live in this darkness, can they survive the wait

where do we send dreams when they faulter, when they fall

when the sky rejects the depth of memory

when the coalition between faith and failure

are no longer cohesive when sunlight greets this skin

when dark is a policeman's greatest fear

Steel Black

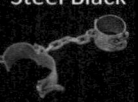

when fear is our favorite companion

we ride with, walk with, live with

America has grown use to neglecting laws

concerning us, to obliterating the black family

the black man when dealing with black bodies

black death, we are still fighting for breath

for a listening ear if only there were black bullets

so we would know when death is coming

when the shadows of time appear over the horizon

attempting to catch black men dragging black skin

to purpose, down destiny lane, we know it is forbidden

to harbor black dreams of black men and black boys

in this land where it is still illegal to be black

My Next Workshop

I would love to tell you

after graduating from High School

four of the five seeds I grew from love

they would tell you what a great dad

I am - or was - or could be

but that isn't the case

what if life had not compiled

these unexplained complications

what if love was able to last

as long as the vows repeated

when we believed better and worse

were just words written down

to sound good for those in attendance

I have to believe

my next writing workshop

will be held in a bedroom - in the house

behind the same locked doors

where they witnessed love

seep through closed windows

escape through cracks in the kitchen tile

puffed as smoke under shingles

all the conversations they don't remember

were buried deep in a well in the back yard

Steel Black

my next writing workshop

will not be written on pages

pens will not be required

we will not use pencils too many lines

have been erased already

we will carve our thoughts into emotions

into unanswered questions

the subject of the workshop will be

when love leaves where does it go

or if love last forever what date did it start

who stamped the expiration

on the unopened package of broken promises

what can force a heart to forget

the struggle of minutes to create days

as you can see workshops only have structure

in the preparation phase, when you are preparing

when you look into the eyes of those ready to listen

you will not be equipped for how listening

sounds close up, you won't be ready

for the echo of memories reverberating through

clinched teeth, where do we go from here

and how do we get there, is there really

a bridge over troubled waters

if so can it hold all the baggage

we have to carry

Rest

Life is life

family is forever

we pray all those we love

will be here until then

but we have known for a while

breath will not always be here to greet us

I grew up with friends that were more brothers

than the blood flowing through our veins

was able to recognize

we all had so many mothers

we respected and loved each one

they whooped us when we did wrong

laughed with us even if we were not funny

or the joke didn't land properly

showed us what was right

believed in us when we didn't

and loved us regardless

our tears today are warranted

every hug is needed

every smile is an I love you unspoken

time is never kind it's just time

it has no bearing on love or family

I love you for life even in the thereafter

Steel Black

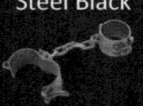

when God calls one of our mothers to rest

we will not agree or understand the why

there are questions we still have

and hugs we need

to help us through this day

there will be no words to explain

no way to measure

how much we miss them

we will gather together

to tell the stories

of how much they

meant to each of us

there will be tears

we will cry overtaken by sadness

we won't know how to say how we feel

how there is a void in the center of our chest

how her absence will affect us

we will not know the answers

but we must celebrate

her leaving here to go home

and understand the time will come

when your job here is complete

or not complete that is up to you

my other mom would always ask me

how I was then wait for the answer

imagine someone loving you enough

to wait for the answer

if you wonder why I marvel at words

why I find great importance

in the structure of sentences

it is because I had mothers like this

who loved me enough to listen

made my thoughts feel worth listening to

would ask questions and wait for the answer

I can't recall the number of times

she would tell Herbert and I

to clean up after cooking French fries

at three in the morning

to cut out that noise

and stop slamming them bones so hard

right now I need every one here to stop

look around you – hug somebody

smile – hug someone else

forget whatever you thought

you were angry about

erase whatever reason

you've held on to that anger

forgive yourself - that's the only way

you can ever forgive someone else

the only thing you must remember

Not Just Alphabets

Steel Black

is Life is life

family is forever

we pray all those we love

will be here until then

but we have known for a while

breath will not always be here to greet us

we have to love one another

as though this breath will be our last

it is not by chance we are sitting here

god brought us together for a reason

I will always be grateful

for everything you've done for me

for helping me to grow into this man I am

for teaching me everyone deserves

to be listened to, every voice matters

I have loved you for life

and will do so even in the hereafter

God has commanded you to rest

may your legacy continue to flourish

may all of your seeds find peace in your going home

we are all here to celebrate your arrival

and to give Thanks and honor

for how you lived

and how you loved us all

when heaven says rest ... rest... Amen

What Is It Worth

I read somewhere it is the drums and bass

replacing the rhythm of hearts in the listening

audience giving a song its worth, others say

they are attracted only to the beat - lyrics

do not matter, for me - it is in the picture's

sounds make, the way tongues maneuver

between teeth, our eyes are not windows

they are portals for vision, our souls are tired

of seeing our demise, there are slices

of skin in my pen, follicles of hair

in these songs, you will not believe

how hard it was to get my ancestors to agree

to let me share me with you, what is it worth

to know, you have done everything you could

gave your all in the effort, I am still

digging up promises left in unmarked

shallow graves, got ghost messaging me

explaining how we have embellished

their stories, turned glory into a mockery

singing songs of hallelujah, how hallelujah

ain't that high, swing low wasn't about

Steel Black

swings or low

got left over ears glued to pages

from those believing poetry

does not require perfect pitch and sacrifice

these days they are killing us like sacrifices

the fatted calf, the families goat

a turkey for dinner

what if history has it all wrong

what if every story told or written

of our days here in America held no truth

for every excuse there is a reason

for every reason there is a cause

for every cause there is purpose

purpose does not come with handles

or edges, corners or written instructions

purpose will not leave you when you leave it

purpose is the first thought you think

but the last thing you know

all my life I have heard purpose will find you

no one ever said you must search for it

no one knows the street, corner or cities

purpose frequents, how can we heal a nation

born of wedlock, we are the bastard children

of a country formed and filled

with bastard children

still struggling to find two fifths

to make us whole

in Alabama there is a museum depicting

all the hangings of blacks in America

the who, where and when

no one will ever be able to explain the why

even now we are still being murdered

in old and new ways - but if death is death

how come here they almost never call it murder

for Native Blacks - blue is a horror story

if we search the genealogical tree

of police in America

I am sure we will find sheets and hoods

white as snow hidden somewhere in their roots

every day new characters play the role of victim

there are no heroes or champions only assassins

the star will always be dressed

in the same blue uniform

badge, gun, taser, lights blaring bright

like that song we would kneel to

instead of placing hands over heart

Not Just Alphabets

Steel Black

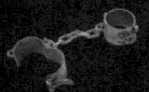

kneeling, praying, hoping they refrain

from issuing more pain

I am beginning to believe

in our communities all they know is pain

no protecting, no serving - just pain

in this unjust system they keep finding

just ways, to systematically kill just us

what is it worth to know

you have done everything you could

gave your all in the effort

while this country still believes

we are two fifths short

of discovering our true worth

Essay

How Dreams Look Close Up

Steel Black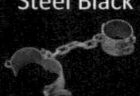

How Dreams Look Close Up

     I remember the day I decided I would go ahead and create my firs poetry cd. The title came to me in a dream "Love Seasons". In my mind, it had the potential of being a global phenomenon. I had visions of all my friends, family and even my mother loving the content. I called Steve and asked when he had time to help with the music and production. Once everything was finalized, I got on a flight, flew to California with so much expectation. Upon arrival, Steve was putting the final touches on a project for a group of rappers. The music was hyped, the beats were banging, the flow was indeed interesting. I don't know why the poet in me listen to words and lyrics more than beats. Anyway, when my turn came they asked me what I would be working on? I told them, an all love poetry cd. I can still remember how hard they laughed. It wasn't the off and on laughter, the roar of their voices was constant. There were three cases on Heineken on ice, we toasted and began to discuss the project out loud with everyone in and out of the studio listening.

     I guess it sounded interesting and no one in attendance had heard anything like that, that is if it went the way of our discussion. No one left a least for the first 12 hours. Dreams take on a whole new personality when more than one person in agreement begins and participates in building it from scratch. The first track was just the introduction, but we had to get it perfect. I think we changed the tempo at least three or four times. Steve laid the track for the drums and Chris sat back strumming his lead guitar as if it was a part of his body. It was a marvelous sight to see, Chris in the zone creating flawless rhythms from scratch. We went over multiple riffs before we found one that felt like it was the perfect fit. Steve picked up the bass and played the coldest bass lick I had heard since I saw Bootsy Collins live. We listened to it two or three times, without hesitation he deleted it and said, "it wasn't right, he could do better". By then I sat with pages in hand looking more visitor than participant. I wasn't amazed but the next time he fingered the bass was absolutely 'PERFECT'. Now, it was my turn to listen and make the words I had written fit between the notes. By then the small room was crowded, I knew I was about to be on blast if the first time they heard me spit something, it didn't go well. So, I sucked up my fear and flowed. It felt good to hear the rappers in the background repeating lines as if they planned to keep and store them for release the next time they were recording.

      But this is about how dreams look close up. Not studio sessions, or rappers, or bass licks, or guitar riffs. Dreams will never look the same when you begin the building process. They won't even have the same taste or texture. Most often they will be so much bigger than you first imagined. We stayed in the studio recording for two days straight only taking short breaks, then getting back to work. For the first day, it seems everyone that was there in the beginning stayed too. Initially I believed it was because the Heineken's were still cold. The point I am trying to make is how much detail do you add to your dream? Do you include possible stages? Is it layered in steps? Or, like me at the time all I could think of was getting the cd completed? Every dreamer must take additional time to analyze not only what product will be produced, but how you expect to package said product. When the work is completed how will you market it and what is the target market. I didn't think of anything beyond creating the cd. It's not flawed to want to create and bring your dream to fruition and not a mistake if you hadn't visualized anything beyond the process. The problem lies in your expectations. How many cd's do you need to sell to break even? Who and where do you plan to place the disc for sale and how much?

      I do not wish to travel back in time because I wouldn't have the lesson earned from this endeavor. Sometimes we fail to see the dream coming true because our expectations appeared long after we put in the work. Dreams work when they are intricately woven with maximum effort, purpose and follow through. If the dream is publishing a book, creating a cd or painting a picture, when you finish the task, you have accomplished the dream. If you expected your friends and family to flock to the party and purchase your finished product then maybe you didn't add enough steps to the dream.

Trust Ink

I've been biting pens instead of poets

originality is the perfect pigment of hope

it is always time with both hands

holding wishes hostage at gun point

hollow thoughts and hollow tips

are detrimental to enlightenment

got a fist filled with faith yet faith

has no color but there is power in believing

if prayers are poems these knees are worn out

I've heard all of our dreams are viewed

in black and white, we've been walking storms

since our arrival, call me colored my color be E

all of the above, I've been a painter since birth

big chief canvas, pencils for paint brushes

my mother told me - imagine I was paper

history can't be whole with most of our

scrolls missing, she said write me new everyday

angels only build rainbows after they are earned

there's a color of ink for everything

keep your broken parts to write with

broken hearts come in black ink

Steel Black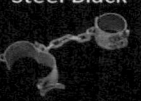

sorrow is a shade tree covered in daffodils

your children and grand children will be

written in pink, the color God made while laughing

remember, memories are never ours to keep

they are the bridge to forgiveness

sadness is a pebbles toss from happier times

pain ain't gon' ever be new again

just recycled, can't wash it clean

pain is dirty - we were born of mud and clay

my grandmother warned me, listening

is the lesson education will never teach us

I am a dollar short of a dollar, a dime

short of a dime you mad that I can't pay

a penny for your thoughts

I've been constructing a body of ink

growing these locs until they connect

to the roots of my ancestors

most know what to say long before you ask them

know what to do long before it's time

in this system built of lies

Truth is all we need to pave a path forward

there are only four things I am sure of:

1. gravity has no effect on patience

2. no matter how much water you pour on concrete

it will not yield a garden

3. tornadoes cannot read street signs

or tell the difference between the numbers

on addresses

4. history told by the victor will never be

the whole truth

we speak of hope as if she wears a crown

peace as if she's mountain tall

freedom, as if a pen could grant us

what we've fought centuries to acquire

from beginning to end

from earth to skin we've been

now and then, women and men

imprisoned for wearing darker skin

I was taught to review, study plus think

my mother told me imagine I was paper

how else would I learn to trust ink

Steel Black

Breathing

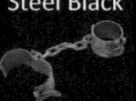

Covid-19 and the men in blue possess similar

undeniable traits, both can render you breathless

force you to visit the nearest hospitals emergency

at least with Covid this country invested billions of dollars

to help expediently discover a cure or create a vaccine

and today a vaccine is on its way

men in blue seem to become embolden with each occurrence

their unions are paid millions of dollars to protect those

when they forget their mission

act in direct opposition to the word protect

after each video, each time their camera malfunctions

we the citizens of dark, of melaninated complexions

of deeper hued skin are offered no recourse

absolutely no satisfaction in America's courts

when we are executed without conscience or cause

eliminated without reason when justice closes her eyes

and cannot see fault in those who smite fear

just by the color of its skin, the way it looks, walks

drives, speaks, policemen used to write tickets

now they bleed the names on obituaries

used to protect and serve now they prepare bodies for funeral service

I can't breathe should never be a sentence

repeated in any community with the consistency

of instant replay, I've heard I can't get my nails done

I can't get my hair did from members of privileged

communities across America because Covid

forced social distancing, forced businesses to close

but never I can't breathe, imagine you rush your child

to the hospital once a week for the various ailments

broken arm, broken clavicle, broken back, broken neck

and not one doctor, orderly or nurse

identifies it as abuse, labels you the abuser

no one calls child protective services

attempting to save the life of the child

I do not believe this scenario is possible

doubt anywhere in the confines of these united states

a neighbor, store clerk, bus driver, emergency care facility

would not sound the alarm if a parent caused harm

left visible bruises on an innocent child

who do you call when bullies, assassins, when police

when the Klu Klux Klan burns a cross on your lawn

when assassins park a cruiser in your grass

when blue and red lights burn brightly on your street

who do you call, when guns are drawn and you're just walking

Steel Black

when tasers are out because you failed to use a turn signal

how criminal has this skin become, how fearful are these dreadlocks

how monster do you consider this skin given me at birth

my throat is not a shotgun, my words are not weapons

my body whatever size it may be is not an explosion

waiting to happen, not a thing you should be afraid of

the new not guilty plea is, 'I feared for my life'

as the suspect ran in the opposite direction

I thought it was a weapon as he talked on his cell phone

believed holding a sandwich was waving a gun

how often have we one way tripped, when our intentions

were to make it back home, when we say support black business

who knew black funeral homes should sell stock

would be the next Apple, Amazon, bit coin

if we had excess dollars to invest in the stock market

the average person takes approximately twenty thousand

breaths per day, in our community almost everyday

at lease once a week on a replay of some lost video

on some small market news station, on Instagram

Facebook Live, on cell phone videos across this great divide

someone wearing this same skin

their breath, their breathing for no just reason

will always come up short

Confessions of an Ink Pen in Witness Protection

some writers fail to comprehend

why I quit mid stroke

why I am brand new and stop writing

immediately after they begin

no one ever asked me if I cared what you write

will it matter how tight or lose you hold me

can I read, do I have feelings

are these real emotions leaking from my tip

can pens cry, are those black, blue or red tears

truth is, we have been crying before we were quills

before they begin dipping our heads into bottles

forcing us to write the unthinkable, a broken preamble

a constitution with the citizens who greeted settlers

welcomed pilgrims, who lived here, whose country It was

from the very beginning missing from its paragraphs

how do you describe a whole person as three fifths

as if each one were deformed, born with

an arm, leg or some major body part absent

a ships ledger omitting proper names, ages

origin, tribe any means of tracing families

back to where they were stolen from

Steel Black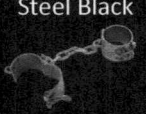

a police report reversing blame and cause

other policemen standing against a blue wall

holding pens hostage to synchronize lies sent to a grand jury

no one has inquired if I remember all the stories

embellished, created for shade, autobiographies

that must be someone else's tale of greatness and grandeur

does it hurt when others use me as the scape goat

for crimes I watched them commit

while they carried me around in jackets and pockets

expecting me not to pay attention

to their short comings, short cuts

falsified documents, back alley agreements

as if people are pages of blatant disregard

I've laid flat as your gavel pounded loudly

giving defendants years for a signature, cash

contract, plea deal, country club membership

every pen in motion shares memories

with every pen that ever moved

we pens don't have secrets, do not know how to lie

we bear witness to centuries of lies and centuries of truth

I have trembled in my barrel writing lyrics

as singers, rappers and poets held me tightly

penning raps, songs, verses to sonnets, prose, poems

words and verses I grimaced composing

I have attempted to unwrite letters

to love ones, to family, some to whom

it may concern, others to whoever finds this

diaries, self-proclaiming nonsense

no one ever asked me if I cared what I am used for

do I possess scars from past fingers

can pens comprehend the passing of time

we usually do not share all the things we know

I'm am just tired of being used for ill gotten goods

by those without hearts, without good intentions

what if we all became overwhelmed

every pen depressed, overtaken with emotions

from ages and centuries of human neglect

what if we only wanted to write truth

only wrote authentic sentences defining

human behavior, penned your true intentions

the real and unedited emotions of the holder

what if humans can only write what we tell them

I am here, hiding in witness protection

to tell you things may not always be the way

you've grown accustomed, used to, fond of

maybe soon we pens and paper will join in rebellion

Not Just Alphabets

Steel Black

an uprising, forcing each of you to reveal

all the secrets you've been hiding

between the lines of code you've written

in each song, each rap lyric, each poem

tell me why no one ever though of asking us

can we read, do we have feelings

is it really ok to keep forcing us to write

the unthinkable, to write words

you failed to believe yourself

Lost In Time

there are mirrors of memories

reflections of yesterday's

trapped in a cluster of tomorrow's

where tortured spirits linger

no one really knows how it works

where ancestors go

when rest is unavailable

how a grave is not a bed of roses

how tombstones are too heavy

for spirits to move

how a funeral can never be

a so long or a good bye

how tears are never wasted

crying has to be the reason

we have ducts in our eyes

instead of damns

what if loved ones lost

huddle by the masses

in a void of time set aside

for remembrance

what if there are no

memory markers

for our memories to mark

Steel Black

what happens if we can't remember

it doesn't mean

time has failed to matter

or our thoughts are broken

do we blame ourselves

when forgetting gets hard

or becomes too easy

how does echoes work

who is charged with repeating

words screamed in the direction

of mountains or clouds

hoping heaven is listening

what if listening is learning

if so, what are you listening to

and who are you teaching

what if every repetitive sound

is a cry for help from someone

somewhere we can't see

what if the only words we hear

are those we are willing to let in

to let go – to repeat as an echo

what if love is an echo when it doesn't

come back will we consider it not love

where does love go when another's heart

is unavailable, when it becomes impossible

to salvage moments

you deemed cherish able

is there a sacred sound

a secret hello or goodbye

we save and savor

in the mirrors of our heart

what if hearts are mirrors

what if memories are mirrors

reflecting only what we want

only what sits directly in front of us

how can we move beyond

the barriers we've built

to keep love safe, what if love

is not supposed to be safe

somewhere there is a cluster

of tomorrows hiding the pain

of our yesterdays

no one really knows how it works

where ancestors go

when rest is unavailable

how a shallow grave

forces their memories

to remain above ground

how funerals are for those

above ground and not below

Not Just Alphabets

In The Garden of Cotton

Steel Black

tears of injustice

may as well be lost echoes

no matter the century

the words are the same

our garden of cotton

will never be flowers

even bathed in rivers of blood

it will remain beautiful white cotton

negro spirituals now have beats

loud drums and overpowering bass

can never drown out the slave in us

the last time we united

we were being prodded and drug

from the under belly of ships

shackled closely wrist to wrist

memories too painful to revisit

our unity these days

is measured five bales at a time

stacks on stacks are simply bales on bales

loaded onto box cars, in Lamborghini's

shipped out of black communities

before anyone notices

we possess the power to save ourselves

but we wait for that good ole by and by

it doesn't matter how large the mansion

it is still surrounded by gardens of cotton

plush acres of green meadows

are easily grown after placing new dirt

over cemeteries, confiscated land

unmarked shallow graves and fields of cotton

when there are no more prayers only whispers

when the darkness of our skin knows no light

when skin color attracts more bullets than empathy

when pleads for justice still go unnoticed

in this war for equality there is no remedy

or combat for pain, if time was a mirror

how many times would the deaths of our sons

fold in on itself, slogans are simply words

hiding so far behind hastags they become

invisibly silent, crop circles are footprints

left by the spirits of our ancestors

searching in circular patterns

for free promised more than a century ago

after being told to leave

the only home they ever knew

they were property often worth

more than the dirt used to rest their heads

I am sure of it, every person who escaped

Steel Black

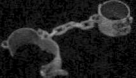

the projects, prison, hood, corner

should have paid a toll for leaving

a tax for community support

left foot notes for fans, family

for those wishing to do the same

there are cotton pickers

in our DNA that refuse to let us be

if freedom was a wheel

its missing a wagon

its spokes are broken

its movement ceased long ago

cannot remember the direction traveled

whoever said the bye and bye

was sweet

still have the husk of cane

stuck in their teeth

Dressing for Church

it should be harder today than ever before

harder to close our eyes and not still see

not know, claim forgetful, believe it accidental

we built it - one just like theirs, outside and inside

as close as we could recall probably white on the outside too

we were taught how great, how good and pure white is

we built it, the First African Baptist Church in North America

first black ownership, we got keys, can lock and open doors

whenever we choose, we are still fighting amongst ourselves

everybody wants to be the leader, still battling to be heard

to speak, to have our name on something as founder

records cannot keep it straight, always pointing fingers

changing the story, no one said how much we want to be like them

how years later our memories will mimic their movements

think we will pick Sunday - just like they did, call it sunrise

break of day, morning worship, call it Sunday school

ain't gone let no one hush us no more, no more whispering

passing notes, dancing to no music, no more shucking and jiving

no more hiding all that hurt, all that bad and beatings

behind a smile and a nod, behind all that quiet like we used to

it began in 1773 organized in 1788 at least that is what the records say

Steel Black

imagine seeing and hearing it for the first time, in all its magnificent

splendor, pretty dresses, heals, petty coats, nice hats, suits

shirts to match, buttoned to the top, shoes all spit shined

socks same color, cannot see no holes in them

we learned to tie ties while watching massah tie nooses

same slip knot, same over under, did not want it to be loose

needed it to be restricting only thing missing is the tree

have to wonder, what the first sermon was, who picked it

which passage did it come from, was it

this is what amazing grace sounds like

could have been - look how far we have come

maybe just yesterday we did not know no better

swing down people and take this chariot ride

how about Daniel in the den with them lions

or maybe Shadrack nem' standing in the furnace

with that fire, we been in the fire, been in the fire

a bunch of times, every time they swung one of us

from them high branches, we eventually landed in the fire

cannot talk about that right now, while we are

dressing for church, imagine how proud everyone

in attendance had to be I can see it, a black man

in a black suit, with a black book , with a black choir

yelling how close we getting to that free

maybe every sermon was not about free

but I bet there was something about free in every sermon

started long before the church got here, I heard

after George Leile got him some free, he started baptizing

and ordaining folk, in 1788 Marshall and Bryan

organized the church built a space underneath the floor

cut little holes in it for air in the shape of the

African prayer symbol, read it was one of the stops

in the underground railroad – a safe house for slaves

for fugitives still today we be dressing for church

do not know why we ain't going why we do not say

what we need to say when we are together

how we gone get that crooked out of our communities

how we gone straighten up and live right, the black church

was the first place a black man could be a man, first time

he could speak out loud, hold his head high, scream

if he wanted to and no one ran back and told massah

did not think he was trying to escape, nobody told us

Reverend Love one of the pastors from this church

started the movement that established Savannah State University

and helped with Morehouse College, bet you did not know

when that church split it formed some of the most iconic

churches in the south birthed some of the most profound

Steel Black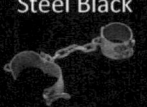

speakers, organizers and activist even Raphael Warnock

won the in the Senate seat in 2021 runoff in Georgia

still got a lot of free in his sermons, like Martin

like Vernon Johns, Robert Pollard like every black man

that stood in the pulpit at Ebenezer, if not for The

First African Baptist Church there would be no Dexter Avenue

no Ebenezer, no bus boycott, no march on Washington

no marchers on the Edmund Pettus Bridge following Martin

as he turned around after the prayer vigil, obeying

a court order not to make the full march across

we been dressing for church for so long

long before Selma, long before Memphis, before the strike

for sanitation workers, now we got churches on street corners

in strip malls, churches with kindergartens, prep schools

and ATM's, big cathedral churches larger than castles

some congregations larger than small cities, some of them

have four and five services on Sunday mornings

we got churches in every neighborhood

I doubt any of them included spaces, hidden rooms

for slaves or fugitives, cannot underground railroad

no more, there would be no safe place for it

even if we needed it to be, we still dressing for church

still ain't going, how can we grow black men

without a safe space, without the truth, without

writing our own scriptures, without memorizing

verses taught us by ancestors, without carving the laws

of black living into existence, when is the last time

you wore your Sunday's best to a Sunday meeting

to a church service that was not a funeral

not a memorial service to hear the good news

a sermon on the mount, the three wise men

water into wine, a lesson you can carry

one you can share, we still dressing for church

a lot of us still ain't going

Not Just Alphabets

Steel Black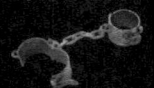

Five Generations From Here

I remember Frank Street in South Dallas

the red and grape berry trees in the front yard

I remember happiness just because we were happy

no one told us we were struggling

I remember dinners with family on my mother's side

dominoes, music, all-night parties on my father's

Charles was not my father's father

he was the man who raised them - all of them

I have much respect for men who pick up steps

left by those whose ladder could not reach the top

for whatever reason could not carry the load

walked with pride and honor never looking back

maybe there are stepfathers

but no such thing as stepchildren

I am named after my mother's father

who passed away before I was born

five generations from here is an eternity, a destiny

a remanufactured journey impossible travel

without help, an unpaved road I may need a ship

to maneuver these rocks, this paved over life

of muddy waters, I don't know much

I just know we were happy

no one told us we were struggling

there is a struggle trying to find a connection

attempting to bridge a history purposely removed

to a truth no one wants to hear

I know for sure my grandfather's father was a slave

my grandmother's mother was a slave too

it is not necessary to go far from here to find entrapment

servitude, to discover why free cannot be felt, spelled

walked, mimicked, found before now

this is the same battle five generations later

same fight, same militia, same police

same government, same laws

same gerrymandered districts, same confederate officers

give me your huddled masses that liberty or death

thing didn't include us, we've waited more than

seven generations to tell our seeds no more

tell our parents no more, grandparents no more

we've suffered more subtractions from rights than additions

more deletions of freedoms than add-ons

and you wonder why five generations from here

is a feat no one can master while we still have masters

or overseers, bounties, still look like slaves

Steel Black

like our education

did not teach us the Preamble

like we have never read

the constitution nor the amendments

like we still running for that illusive free

I Albert, son of Jimmie, son of Charles, son of Birdie

daughter of Albert, can only travel so far

down this family tree before the roots disappear

so five generation from here is a place

I know nothing about but need to know

the truth is... if you do not know

where you come from ...

we all know those words oh so well

Water

I read somewhere

a drop of water and a tear drop

have the same weight

bare the same properties

there are at least four elements

hidden from the periodic table

in hopes men will never discover

the parts of themselves

they were taught to overlook

told was just dead weight

there has to be a section of our brains

broken into two list

acceptable and completely unacceptable

when you know the facts

over seventy percent of our body

is made of ocean

its better if we don't know why

hide the questions we never cared to ask

years ago in a conversation

with his friends I heard my father say

men are not supposed to cry

I always believed

it had something to do balance

Steel Black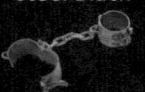

it was the way the male species

kept emotions and love

safely separate, two heart beats

away from falling

the first time I cried

I knew… my father meant

men have no control

over how much water released

how loud the wailing can get

how your arms will resemble

lifeless stems, lay limp as branches

who lost their tree

the second time I cried

I found out the hard way

my pillow wasn't a swimming pool

a blanket wasn't a good support system

emotions were rivers

sometimes it's impossible

to find your way to shore

one drop of water, one tear

bare the same properties

I doubt any man knows

how to properly use their eyes

the third time I cried

I believed I had emptied

my soul and all the oceans

this small body held

until I studied my bodies

true metabolic composition

I am built of

twenty seven gallons of tears

twenty four pounds of skin

there is a small pond resting

in the core of me

once I thought I emptied my ocean

through the corners of my eyes

thought my soul had escaped

from the reality of losing love

I discovered it takes ninety thousand

nine hundred and twenty two

tears to form a gallon

one bucket holds approximately

five gallons of pain

 maybe instead of clouds

tears should be measured

in elephants or mountains or galaxies

my father is no longer with us

so I can't ask him what he meant

all I know is we have ducts

instead of dams

Not Just Alphabets

Steel Black

the seventy percent thing is true

how else can men grow

if we fail to water the seeds in us

and women will always be

the best part of us

the part we will never truly

understand

I must conclude

she had to be an island

I somehow landed on

by accident

Wanna Write No Mo

I don't wanna write no mo black poems

no mo poems about being black

it is similar to not being able to distinguish

night from day only knowing night is night

I do not know where it appears in the bible

what color the angels are, you can bet

even the angels do not want to be black

they can see from heaven the hell we go through

some nights I catch midnight with a flashlight

heard the moon beg the sun to not go

I am beginning to believe the color black

is afraid of being black

I just want to drive and not be scared

shop for food and clothes and not be followed

walk or jog peacefully and not look suspicious

I do not wanna be looked down on when I am taller

have to look up from the ground for no reason

shouldn't police have a reason or is it ok

to shoot for no reason, I know my rights

but black rights are not equivalent to white rights

someone asked me why is white privileged

Steel Black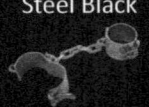

it is impossible to explain why white is privileged

in a black poem it would make no sense

when the Senate sets precedence during

the term of a black president

and the precedent is no longer in effect

when white privilege is serving in the white house

we may not agree but that would be a perfect example

I can't tell you why white is privileged

I just know whites get to ask questions when stopped

finish their sentences in the presence of police

any sound from blacks is considered resisting arrest

I don't wanna write no mo black poems

it is hard to tell white dust from black dust

when bones rust or find truth in facts with blind trust

why black truth and white truth are not the same truth

look at history – history has a unique way

of determining black from white

black history only has twenty-eight days

white history has more than four hundred years

reconstruction was the period when blacks could freely vote

many held office in congress and senate

this lasted fourteen years, Jim Crow abolished

all the progress made during reconstruction

and lasted more than one hundred years

maybe privilege is a gift of time

what if we changed the statement from people died

to give us the right to vote, to people were killed

assassinated because of voting - would it matter

to those not committed to the process, it happened

we do not know for sure how many times it occurred

there are estimates of the number of blacks murdered

by hangings in America - who kept tabs, who held the abacus

is there a secret ledger, why did it take until December

of twenty eighteen to pass the Justice for Victims of Lynching Act

the civil war ended in eighteen sixty-five and here we are

still fighting for rights promised in amendments and clauses

General Robert E. Lee a member of the confederate army

lost the battle of Gettysburg, years later

there are statues erected in his honor

giving him the status of hero, maybe white privilege

is allowing traitors to be written in historical documents

however the writer wishes them to appear

why is being black so different than being white

is it the exclusion of people with melanin

deliberately omitted from its founding documents

I don't know why black have no privilege

Steel Black

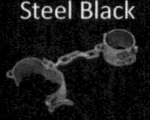

why this color doesn't come

equipped with rights

I believe America thinks we look better

in shackles than suits, better in stripes than jeans

better in the back seats of cruisers

explaining white privilege in a black poem

makes no sense, it is as if trying to explain

why deserts are not beaches

and they are both full of sand

or why the sky is not made of water

but it is blue like the ocean

I don't wanna write no mo black poems

it is problem enough being black, educated

knowing how to speak, write, the last thing

America needs is another black poet

if you ask why blacks have no privilege

maybe privilege is a luxury and cannot be attached

or given to those once shackled

to fields or best used as free or cheap labor

I don't wanna write no mo black poems

even the color black carry's a night lamp

it is worn out and weary from the struggle

of being black

Wake Up

what if I told you - showed you

proved to you without a doubt

there are ghost - restless spirits

shaking the cages of our days

we are still haunted by the swinging

ropes of history held together by lies

twisted by white wig wearing quills

pasted on documents we were never

meant to read , plastered in hard covered

Dewey Decimal coded books

Me, I am just a poet attempting to dig up

uncover – reveal bits and pieces of truth

that has been hidden, kept secret for centuries

you really want to know why we do

what they do, why our actions mirror our captors

we only know what they taught us

only believe what they allowed us to read

I am just a poet – trying to write enough truth

so you can see yourself, dark skin beautiful

hair like God planned , there is a native in you somewhere

a chained-up warrior wishing for a way out

Steel Black

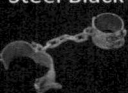

hoping you will look close enough

to see your great grandmother's

and your great grandfather's eyes

blinking an SOS as you look in the mirror

there is a message you need to hear

my ancestors told me to tell you

yours are waiting for you to wake up

waiting for you to listen - to hear

we are better than this

better than they say we are

better than we've been

so much better than

we've been to each other

there is a reason most

of the clothes we wear

are made from the same

cotton they were forced to pick

their specific design and color

is to make you forget the struggle

every hurricane is sent as a warning

a sign you've gotten too comfortable

in your captor's clothes

wearing your captor's hair

living in your captor's shack

thinking you've arrived

this is the message my ancestors told me

to tell you, yours are waiting for you

to wake up, waiting for you to listen

sleep is for those who have nothing better

to do than rest, those who found

too much comfort in hiding from this struggle

there is a native in you somewhere

a chained-up warrior wishing for a way out

our ancestors are shaking the cages of our days

attempting to frighten you awake

wake up because we are better than this

we must be better to each other

than we've ever been

if we ever plan to see our way clear

fight our way through

there are ghost - restless spirits

sending a storm, a tornado, a hurricane

to un comfort your comfort

wake up

Not Just Alphabets

Steel Black

Come Mourning

we will often not speak of the gone

of friends and family for reasons

beyond the control of our hearts

who we said whatever goodbye

our eyes would allow

if it were just my heart buried in sorrow

it would never matter to the masses

in America due to Covid -19 we all

have lost more than four hundred thousand

friends, love ones, family, associates

who will sing come morning

will amaze our grace or streets pour gold

who can touch our souls when

eyes leak at the thought of missing a touch

we will never feel again, if it is grace

that brought us this far, why did it not

bring them along, it is impossible to sing

when the song, when the melody is missing

come mourning who will cry with me

who will sing of days no more coming

come mourning I will cry for you

I will weep for those who shared

their last breath with nurses and doctors

when family could only sit alone

when quarantine forbade us to family

come mourning we will remain here

alone, by grace, by faith sharing tears

of remembrance

Steel Black

Fractured Mindset

my thoughts are lost journals

transcribed in midnight shade and black sunshine

spiral bound, twisted blank pages

of stolen poems written in reverse

I am two wishes short of the last thing I hoped for

one sprint and two steps from reaching my destination

it is impossible to walk the bridge underneath

the oceans river or the trail that leads from here

to nowhere in particular

I am three breaths short of an inhale

eight winks from seeing clearly footprints in the sand

I am an uncloudy sky raining sand

on a forest fire sparked by lightning strikes

I am a no handed scribe taking pains dictation

you have no idea how it feels to have to

remove your arms before raising your voice

I am a windstorm filled with dust

a dust storm filled with smog

a rainbow made of mud flooding my dirty mind

I have memories left over no one remembers

I am broken promises clawing holes in the pockets

of my favorite jacket there is a thimble

stuffed with straw I am using to knit myself whole

I am broken pieces of broken pieces

fruit with no tree, a puzzle missing its picture

created a road map in rhymes, wrote tears

in sonnets fed a multitude with words

formed of two haiku's and 5 slam poems

preached a sermon on a mount of severed branches

baptized my mind with a glass of dirty water

felt the echo crawl into my throat before

the beginning of sound , what came first

the mountain or the mole hill

the flood or the rain, the stars or the darkness

the hurt or the love, the flames or the smoke

the fire or the match, the rib or the woman

I am lies told, truth undiscovered

a forbearance of prayer awaiting freedoms reprise

I am flat earth on a round axis

a distant moon we have never had a chance to meet

a snowstorm in the dessert a heat wave

in the polar ice caps , I am lies in school

I am learning to untell myself

truth taking faiths dictation

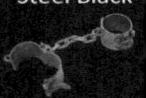

Steel Black

halo's secured by duct tape

I am reasons reason, logics logic

a poets pen filled with misremembers

a cracked frame holding a fractured mindset

a clock with both hands removed

waiting until tomorrow, I am patience

painting patches of purpose in pictures

I am pictures of purpose

painted by patience's patients

we are all wearing truths straitjackets

society built for us at birth

we are wishes strapped to hopes wings

searching for a distant blessing

we are blessings

disguised as friends

disguised as poems

disguised as pens

we are writers

holding a thimble of straw

hoping we are able to write

to truth, to knit ourselves whole

History Updated

it maybe time for us to stop

being embarrassed, stop being afraid

around those who fear the truth

being black in America has become

an instant apology, a mouth full

of I am sorry because slavery ended

so abruptly after 246 years, sorry we are now

demanding you let us matter

grant us human, sorry we are requesting

payment for our forefathers

full unabridged compensation

for atrocities suffered, for unbinding contracts

for inventions borrowed

for abandoning your seeds, for child support

for thousands of children you left with no last name

demanding recompense for every year of labor

without equitable reimbursement, without charging

overtime, holiday pay, workman's compensation

unpaid vacations, sick leave, maternity leave, on the job injuries

I have witnessed us apologizing for physical abuse, beatings

hangings, for the murders of black boys, men and women alike

Steel Black

maybe we should stop having all this resisting arrest

in our voices, the weaponizing of sounds escaping our throats

maybe we should handcuff ourselves to insure attending officers

will not have to shoot us in the back as they fear for their lives

not be forced to falsify documents, edit the police video

will not be forced to have their union representatives change

arresting documents, will not have to choose members for a

grand jury, here it is, we are living in the twenty first century

we still cannot tell the difference between a police siren

and the churning, grinding engine of a slave ship, cannot

distinguish between a sweat box and a jail cell

have we learned nothing from the sitting at lunch counters

from thousands of warnings from sundown towns

from a million men marching, poll taxes, stop and frisk

jury tampering, looking suspicious, turning the other cheek

we should have noticed how far freedom was from here

by the number of times Harriet had to buy shells for her shotgun

when a peaceful march on Washington was met with resistance

when peaceful protesters at Lafayette Square came face to face

with riot control, we should have realized black lives did not matter

when we were bundled and packaged like coffee for unsafe passage

when ships were retrofitted to maximize human cargo

when the number of transports reached over 40,000

by the number of presidents trying to force America to be great again

did we learn nothing from history, did carrying signs

for years and miles not give us strength enough

to withstand the trials time withstood, can we not hear

messages from drums hidden in histories timeline

have we remembered nothing our ancestors taught us

have we forgotten where hurricanes come from

can we not roar life to footprints at the bottom of the Atlantic

we should be able to call for help in the dance of storms

we can repeat the chant of ages requesting spirits of oceans

to rise on America's midlands in the tracks of tornadoes

has history taught us nothing, should we not recognize

the damage and hurt in our communities when we refuse

to view our reflection in the rearview mirror of police squad cars

in the framed portraits of past presidents while sitting in court

waiting for justice's arrival, look how far we have come

from where they started, how freedom seems to be as

far from now as it was from then, how we are still singing

of overcoming, still harmonizing songs of someday

maybe we can learn to chant I am sorry's

into a new revolution, we can no longer remain passive

when truth awaits an awakening, stands in the position

where truth has always stood, maybe, just maybe our children

Steel Black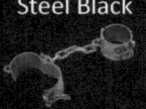

will have more courage than we possess

maybe their children will remember

how long it has taken to get us here

there are tombstones awaiting promises

we made, awaiting a stamp of approval

there are legacies hoping we have the strength

to pull them forward, how many leaders

must we sacrifice before there is

a return on investment, before blood out

is equivalent to blood in, did we learn nothing

from our lackadaisical participation

in the voting process, in our fear of running for office

fear of being accountable for years of inaction

we apologize for our fear of assassination

in a true attempt to expand the road to freedom

as we update history, whose pen

with quote tomorrow

how many voices will echo the truth of now

to this day we still march

we still sing

we still struggle to be free

They Told Me Lies

the Constitution should be

written in crayon with the history

of America a color by numbers

coloring book

I am not for sure how it works

how do you correct a tale of woe

a story made of nothing but imagination

and stolen language of the victor

once upon a time settlers on ships

arrived on the shores, crashed on rocks

lost and disheveled had no idea

how to navigate the land

on which they discovered

and quickly confiscated

don't know how a simple flag

became a declaration of ownership

who penned the lies

how many story tellers did it take

to become four score and seven years

of propaganda, how many tall tales

had to be told to make true

Not Just Alphabets

Steel Black

the indigenous people of this land

gave it away willingly, they should call them

trickies instead of treaties

signatures and handshakes

are the gestures of jesters

don't believe a word they say

do not believe a word written on pages

labeled his story

they told me lies, told us lies

here I am repeating the tale of woe

as if it is the truth and the only tale I know

the story of a stolen people

in a stolen land, speaking a stolen language

why would we tell children any history

the writers should have written in crayon

as if calling a people colored

makes up for servitude

you think no one will notice

how you believe

building a nation of black and white

will automatically include us

in the book of colors

you cannot begin to estimate the damage

think avoiding the conversation

means no payment is necessary

we have been called so many names

America doesn't know who to pay

when negroes, colored people, niggers

Afro Americans, African Americans

ask for reparations

lies are easier to swallow

when we are the main ones

repeating them

Steel Black

The River

there is a river

somewhere next to the dream

I had of you, where it is possible

to rinse away your doubts

filled to the brim with wishes

that could never work on their own

wishes never could

nor can dreams build themselves

we all tend to have more dream than feet

can't run fast enough to keep up

every day I try to make sense

fall from the tips of these fingers

some days it's a trap

I can't pull myself out of

or find my way through

we love to blame hope

when it is always our fault

resting while work needs to be done

eating too much at the wrong time

sitting at the edge of the battlefield

warriors never wait for weapons

warriors are the weapons

this world has been waiting for

you don't need more than you to fight

drum up your warrior find your cause

there is a river somewhere in the bottom

of your belly needs a push to start flowing

can only be fed by the stream of your own

imagination, there are no fish in this sea

it is just the river you must travel

to get to the ocean of your thoughts

better teach yourself to swim on the way

boats could never fit here you are the life raft

if you ever require a raft for your life

drowning in your own purpose

can be considered suicide

your tongue with no faith

is a pin less grenade you can hurt yourself

by speaking too fast if you fail to pay attention

ain't no guide on this path

help doesn't know its way here

I can't tell you anything you don't already know

falling while learning to walk is the way we got here

this is the adult version, you will fall sometimes

Not Just Alphabets

Steel Black

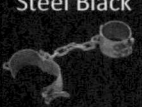

damn near drown in your own river

some days will forget how to swim

will beat yourself up when forced to

retake the class from a lesson you've failed

too many times before, we will all fail some lessons

we thought we knew the solutions to

will damn near drown when we forget

how to paddle, be drug back to the starting line

after believing the race, the fight

this battle was over, if you are still breathing

this battle will never be over

there will be another ocean a little further

off this path you never knew existed

it's hard to soldier up if no one taught you

how to be a soldier, the war usually begins

inside first, you won't hear the gun shots

we love blaming those outside

say it is their fault our river stopped flowing

why our ocean can't be seen

from the chair we are sitting in

wishes were never given legs for a reason

nor can dreams build themselves

and we can't build dreams

until we build ourselves

the earth is round in order to teach us

we will be back in this same spot

in this same place peering across the same bridge

with similar trials soon enough

drum up your warrior find your cause

you won't need more than you to fight

I can't teach you anything

you didn't already know

and I am still struggling to learn

things I believed I already knew

I wish I had some easy to offer you

we are aware easy can't get you nowhere

that's why they call it easy

every day I try to make sense

fall from the tips of these fingers

as usual today it's a trap

at least I am walking these wishes

dragging these dreams, left doubt at the last stop

I will never blame hope, ain't no guide

on this path and you better believe it

when I tell you

help doesn't know its way here

Steel Black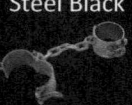

How To Build an Underground Railroad

to build anything you must first

find a starting point

we never know in America where to begin

they keep moving the stories

you know, the in the beginnings

the once upon a times

the fourscore and seven years agos

rewriting their story when there is no his in it

start by reading history

learn who wrote it, whose pen penned

the ink you want to call truth

you need to know necessity denotes

a new underground railroad

is required at this juncture

know who created it and why

or rather what the tracks are made of

how long was and is the journey

how many days, weeks, months did it take

give honor to others who discovered

it was their duty to follow suit

Harriet was the author the founder of the tracks

if cars were used or boxes

whatever you want to call it

they grew however many seats necessary

no sides or walls could be used

no one knew when moving quickly

would be the only thing to keep you alive

she carried a shot gun not for protection

not for enemies from those seeking free

they were not aware in the beginning

the high cost of freedom, she needed a shot gun

to protect from those preferring captivity

over the struggle of getting some free

they know now, living in bondage was so much easier

she said would have freed thousands more slaves

if they only know they were slaves

made nineteen trips over ten years

more than eight hundred miles each

lasting an average of six weeks

it is estimated more three hundred slaves

were led to freedom, she never lost a person

historians write over one hundred thousand

slaves were freed between 1810 and 1850

who knew today, right now

Steel Black

we would need to hitch box cars together

build tracks out of something

out bones scattered about in unmarked soil

out of water still baring footprints left centuries ago

out of branches tired of the painful memories

they grow every spring and forget

each time autumn shows up

there is so much of our blood

wasted on American streets

blood isn't strong enough to build tracks

able to hold anything other than tears

who knew today, right now

we would need to pack hopes and wishes

in crates, load them on trains

that will carry dreamers to a land

where dreams come true

who knew we would have to go underground

to get some free - to take us away from death

from shootings, harassment, cases we didn't deserve

years of incarceration they plea bargained us into

I had a dream I was there

a dream we were there

hiding in the woods, behind trees

near the water, under leaves

huddled close, eyes shut

could not hush the fear in our spirits

quiet the rumble in our bones

I had a dream, dreamed free

was as far from here as it was then

when I awoke

free is further from here as it was then

who knew today, right now, this moment

we would need to hitch box cars together

there are tracks in the arms of dead bodies

left over from drug wars no one wanted to fight

tracks built of brick and mortar

from crack houses, projects, trap houses

only America knows they are all the same thing

there are tracks made of shells left by police

no excuse is needed to shoot us anymore

tracks built of caution tape, of fear

of bodies tased, choked, beaten, hung

tracks built from hate

in our community we are still the last to know

America doesn't care

they have spent centuries

Not Just Alphabets

Steel Black

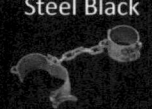

forcing others to build

whatever they thought they needed

consider these facts

they forced the Japanese

to build railroads out of steel

the Cubans and Haitians to build

railroads out of tobacco

out of stalks of sugar

forced the slaves to build railroads

out of cotton, out of children

out of women, built railroads

out of everything they love

built tracks out of confederate flags

soldiers, confederate generals

confederate presidents,

out of slave traders, bounty hunters

who knew today, right now, in this moment

we would need an underground railroad

to take us from these troubles

and get us some free

Promises

There are promises misspelled

on the back of the Constitution

written in the language of presidents

slave masters, I mean investors

who continued the slave trade

there are bodies buried in cotton fields

beneath mansions, government buildings

Skyscrapers, some were made aware

before the foundation was finished

construction was never halted

it did not matter

neighborhoods were created

where plantations once stood

on the hallowed ground

of slavementaries, the cemeteries of slaves

their names will not be remembered

many parents across America are not aware

of the sacred grounds their children play

there are promises carried by storms

whispered through time hidden somewhere

in the wheels of stagecoaches

Not Just Alphabets

Steel Black

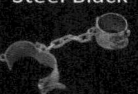

the wood and stone of houses

on dirt roads that used to be

the thirteen colonies

our broken promises go way back

to the beginning, before we could read

write or hold our heads up

while listening, we are asked to forget

opportunities we never had

the rights to reach

I cannot recall one promise

America has kept

America will quickly find new labels

to make you responsible

for their short comings

"Indian giver, lazy, cheap labor

beaner, porch monkey, spic

spook, gooks, slant eyes,

they have a name for us all

but not one to call themselves

America knows we like our promises

boxed up and resold

for one hundred and thirty years

Aunt Jemima on front

uncle Ben unapologetically

on the back, you know

back of the bus, store, restaurant

line, back of the constitution

back past the usual amendments

to those added so much later

the 13th and 14th and so forth

America knows how we like our promises

laced front with a little baby hair all 1492

bundled with ole glory on our backs

as if we have been claimed as property again

we know promises

as if they were the legs, ankles

chained together for remembrance

for clarity, we've been told

change will not come willingly

will not leave when asked

we have come this far

by sure grit and faith

imagine being or becoming

the embodiment of what

our grandmothers say we should be

there are secrets in sand

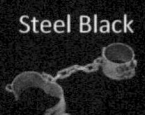

Steel Black

we will never recover

footprints of us walking alone

nobody carrying us over

the threshold of time

here we are needing

more friends than opposition

more family than these

connected DNA strands

will allow us to share

there is a message, somewhere

written on the underside of dirt

on the inside of boxes

locked tight with six ten finished nails

help carved in the ceiling

with broken fingers of sons

gone to soon

Inheritance

I've been walking toward freedom

since I started to crawl

I am no closer today

than my great grandfather

or the many black men before him

there are plans in the plans

other leaders sketched before leaving

targeted assassinations or not just targets

the day we call assassinations assassinations

is the day we move a step closer

to the realization

not all of us will make it to shore

even if you could swim

blood is thicker than water

breathing under blood

is not a thing that could actually happen

I've been calling a spade a spade

since I inherited these hearts

sons and daughters are the gardens

we are sworn to grow to fruition

turn the other cheek was carved into stone

Steel Black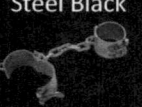

but not a rock

we should continue to carry

my father explained

forgetfulness is not possible

when all you have known is centuries of pain

we know pain - like family - like it is ours to keep

like it is the horse we road in on

like it is the clothes on our backs

the napps in our hair

we act as if we don't know no better

like we were never taught black manners

like my legs were not popped

when my mother thought I misbehaved

last time I slept I had a dream

all mountains were mole hills

the tops of them missing as if chopped off on purpose

insuring we will never see or reach the top

the deepest thought possible was passed on

by a president with the vocabulary of a fifth grader

I talk with a limp, sound as if my words

are a cross too heavy for one man to bear

how do you drag a history of burdens

away from sons unaware their families curse

is to protect others from the burdens

time has tried to rid itself of since the first full moon

since the midnight sky pregnant with the sun

gave birth to the breaking day

who do I ask questions or rather how

tell me how or when do I ask

who choose white as the color of skin

for a people closer to pink

could have chosen white because red was already taken

Christopher brought it with him upon his arrival to the islands

the Pilgrims carried it in the blade of their flags

when they discovered a new land already inhabited

the American tradition of taking

is how this country was founded

there were presidents who perpetuated hate

through the continued participation of slavery

maybe the choice of white was for purity and kindness

all the things America wished it were

but we know better – we've seen the dark side

of a nation that only has a dark side

maybe we will find freedom when we lumber jack

every tree that replaced its bark with skin

every branch still branding scattered pieces of rope

Steel Black

every remnant of prejudice

still brandishing its smile

on government property with traitors

every state or city still flying ole dixie

as if it doesn't resemble a hanging or death

each time it waves in the wind

maybe we will know freedom

when we carve enough tombstones

on all the graves

we never knew were graves

when we place markers on the ocean floor

in remembrance of those who refused

to give up their freedom

yeah we know pain

we know pain - like family

like it is ours to keep

it greets us every morning

tucks us in bed each night

we know pain

like it is the clothes on our backs

the breath we may not be

afforded tomorrow

we know pain

because it has been with us

since cotton, since cane

since tobacco, since America

began keeping tabs on third graders

since money for justice depended on

black men being incarcerated

since we have to take to the streets

just to get justice

for murdered of women of men

yeah, we know pain

we know pain like family

Steel Black

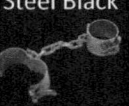

Just Answers

Imagine

there was no apocalyptic event

the dinosaurs laid themselves down to rest

discovering bones needed to be accompanied

by a story we keep telling the story

keep making it different each time

what if a group of writers loved their hood

stayed there happy with writing and home

until we labeled it a renaissance a rebirth of sorts

after returning from travels abroad, new countries

that were also fighting for us offering new freedoms

we marvel at magicians knowing all too well

there is no such thing as magic, slights of hand

are slights we know anything about

I wonder how many answers we let rest

on our tongue before sharing them as truths

how many times will you be the source of knowledge

holding answers we know nothing about

there are questions in my pen

I may never write the answers or even pen the questions

we are not aware of what belief feels like

until we believe in something we have felt

we have a bad habit of repeating answers

even when we are not sure

of where said answer originated

how are we capable of such great failures

when we have been blessed with much potential

is grace a skin color, a hair style, is grace a woman

should we hold her as holy, as the gift

the most high intended connecting man to heart

and heaven, what if man was formed

from the rib of a woman

how much unlearning must we unteach ourselves

Keepsakes

every day I am writing

love's keepsake

with a pen filled with borrowed time

in the hallowed halls of a tomorrow

slowly seeping into yesterday

you wonder why I write

my pages are where

huddled masses congregate

hoping ink will be their voice

even when they speak in thunder

where other people see ghost

I hear whispered verses of dead poets

demanding I get it right

spell checking my autocorrect

screaming scribe

write what I told you

what I should have written

while my hands still had breath

write that thing no one wants to hear

but everyone needs to stop and listen to

write a cry for help or a helpful cry

write that wish the young man gave you

when he didn't even know he was wishing

write what your mother told you

what your father wanted to say

write an apology to battered women

a list to heal the spirits of abandoned babies

write a constitution that works

carve a prayer in a hope

in a song through a poem

shout a picture on a page

no one has seen

create a thought that makes ideas

perform an exorcism on imagination

use your bones if you have to

you better get this right

most attentions can't span

beyond the perimeters of their cellphones

write a cellphone poem

able call the inattentive

leave a text message in their voice mail

write an anecdote – an ink vaccine

to old and new pandemics

write a virus to eradicate viruses

write a solution for hunger

for starving artist who need verses

write survival a list of items

write a list of items to survive

Steel Black

write a sun for daydreamers

dreaming of days spent wishing

instead of working to make wishes happen

write a cure for sadness

a prescription for happiness

a bandage for hearts no longer

connected to the body it lives in

write a splint for broken promises

a bridge from now to then

I got pens taking medicine

wearing mask through this pandemic

I got pages replanting themselves

knowing they can be trees again

I know I must write what they told me

write the things I know need to be sound

how do we write enough substance to keep

or keep enough substance to write

I keep writing keepsakes

praying the sounds will matter

to more than me

we are all one wish from hope

one step away from fruition

no matter what we think or say

we got to get this right

Lessons In Sound

my father taught me

there are no safe words

I am sorry does not have the power of removal

it cannot wash away blemishes or stains

apologies are a last ditched effort at clemency

an eyes down, open palm internal act of attrition

how do you ask for mercy or pardons

when circumstances are beyond description

every word capable of surrender of decapitation

our tongues and teeth will not block

the worst messages escaping

the void in the center of our face

no one can master thought or sound

we rely on echoes to prove our theories valid

an echo is someone, anyone

we said something to repeated back to us

as a sign we have said something of significance

something worthy of them listening

I know people who would rather sign

only if it was a language they knew

or those who skip hello go straight to goodbye

Steel Black

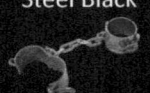

no longer wasting time introductions and small talk

leave no pigments in the big picture

I'm learning to speak in tears or hugs

or screams or smiles

our ability to be empathetic has diminished

since we were last in captivity

poetry is such a traumatic disorder

I am sure the author of those songs

sung in circles, whispered in shanty huts

hummed in the blistering sun

suffered from PTSD or some disease unnamed

for centuries doctors have searched for a cure

we depend on some form of physical vibration

to explain our purpose

humans are considered to have the highest

level of intelligence of all the species on this planet

yet we seldom display a fraction of responsibility

for the carnage and devastation hiding in our closets

we have spaces in our hearts off limits to friends and family

there are plots of bones no one will ever find

there are those whose ideas have been ravished and torn

just for thinking of sharing, unifying or connecting

I have left words in places sound has been banned for years

there is a metronome our feet move to

lodged in the center of our chest

stumbling gracefully will never be a calypso

never be considered dancing

we have pockets filled with

incomplete sentences

fingers bandaged from writing or typing

messages we will never read

there are secrets in our shoes

metaphors void of description

thoughts lying in wait

until we surrender to heightened expectations

our tongues stagger over alphabets

as if we verbalize sound with feet in our mouths

hum with no lips – listen with ears closed

we are searching for words that are safe

but there are no safe words

my father taught me

I am sorry's are void of power

they cannot remove, replace or deflect

can't clean or wash away

acts preformed or mis remembered

we depend on sounds we make

Steel Black

praying in some way

shape or form they produce

the outcome required

for us to continue to be human

intellect misused will not equal intelligence

maybe a world filled with useless chatter

has aided in global warming

it is essential we connect

and communicate to someone

anyone other than ourselves

what if truth is the only thing

that can keep us safe

the only thing we can use

to save us from ourselves

my father would say

we are crippled crabs with no crutches

and no lumber yard to save us

and believe me

we are all in need saving

Maybe It's Just Me

did you ever think nobody else

sees it like you see it

maybe your eyes are just your eyes

ain't nobody supposed to know

how to see it unless you write it down

unless you a poet and God demanded you speak

gave you a little extra volume

so listeners know it ain't you

ain't your sound - these be God's words

heaven filled my pen with thoughts, now I can't sleep

got me mumbling instead of snoring

eyes won't stay closed even when

I place my hands over them

some mornings I write with my left hand

right hand be scared, fingers shaking like legs

it ain't always safe out here being God's echo

ask T'Challa, ask Marcus, ask Huey

ask any of them left us before we needed them to go

the first three masters of this country

I mean first three presidents, were proud slave owners

America been dealing in bodies before she had casinos

Not Just Alphabets

Steel Black

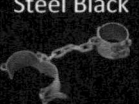

before she kept tally's, before she knew

poets were poeting records jotting shit down

she didn't know, these ain't our fingers

on these hands, ain't our lips, ain't our words

none of this sound belongs to me

America never stopped dealing in bodies

had to keep funding transportation of their investments

to the islands, after she forced all the other countries

to stop, told them they could no longer trade in bodies

could no longer cash in on the sale of skin

wasn't protecting blacks, didn't want anyone else

to know she needed to keep that cane, tobacco

coffee coming cross the water

it ain't right no more, can't use black bodies

as stock options to raise their shares

commodities and stock prices

she still trading in bodies, some of them black

no gun, no hospital, straight to the coroner

most of them ain't know the war was ongoing

been ongoing since before nigga killings became a sport

maybe it's just me who think, every time I see a policeman

riding in the car alone the ghost of Jim Crowe

be riding shotgun, I believe police be keeping

trophies a spent shell casing, a splotch of blood

ask these attorney generals

why they can't seem to see murder in them videos

in them back shootings, in them knees

them choke holds, them no knocks

them new city hangings didn't know Sam Houston

and Jim Bowie already reincarnated

slave traders, bounty hunters, back in the body business

both wearing blue, badges, guns, the same

ole protection and privilege why you think

the present master of this dirt fighting to keep

military bases named after traitors, keep them

statues standing, forcing the wind behind ole glory

to keep blowing, want it to keep waving

keep remembering , like we ain't found

the free they promised us

I been checking, we still ain't found

the free they promised us

right now is just like back then

could be we already in the great again

just didn't know it, nobody told us

you know someone white got to tell us shit

before we believe anything we see is real

Not Just Alphabets

Steel Black

maybe it's just me

maybe I can't get a foothold on these hands

can't force these pens to stop worrying

they keep asking me to write shit

no one wants to hear

want me to write about that WAP

what Kanye running for these days

what he selling now, want to hear that beat

not the drums passing messages

from here to there, cross counties, cross city lines

maybe it's just me

watching over four hundred thousand bodies pile up

thinking this is that great again

pasted on them red hats

nobody knowed they did not care what color

America back in the body business

I'm guessing she never left

if one percent got all the money

how they gone feed all those down line folk

if they ain't want to give up no pennies

why you think they say they out of coins

want you to have correct change

and Covid took your job already

got us just like before

needing a chicken in every pot

I keep thinking like Gil

all this shit happening

while whiteys on the moon

ain't no space program right now

you can't have a space program

and make bodies pile up too

America been in the body business

it just looks a little different

they ain't all black, they did include

other minorities, some elderly

some people with preexisting conditions

maybe it's just me – even regular folk

getting into the body business

I believe if it is new -its new

if it is normal its normal

together they could never be a thing

there is no new normal

no normal that is new

I got questions I was afraid to share

this country must answer questions

that have not been asked

Steel Black

but they know are coming

how much money was made last year

on shirts with the faces of men and women

murdered by police

even the little people in the body business

we ain't doing the killing, just the selling

making death a for profit business

right after one of them slaughtered

we begin to sell them on street corners

In shops across this this country

even in the neighborhoods they used to live

I guess ain't nobody stopped to ask

how much is pain worth, what is

the price of death, should one tee shirt

be able to hold this much blood

what percentage of those funds

went to the family, is it just me

who got these questions

who need these answers

we are just like America counting bodies

making money off those gone too soon

counting live people who wear the faces

of dead people on they chest

maybe its an honor or something

I just ain't caught up with just yet

maybe we learned too good

it is commonplace to do

what master been doing

we keep using the tricks on us

the same tricks master used to trick us

maybe it's just me

I don't know about you

but I'm tired

I no longer want to be

in the body business

Steel Black

Love Poem

she arrived locked and loaded

wasn't prepared to give more than a smile

told me her all was offered as sacrifice

too many times to be considered available

love is a singular walk across fire stones blindfolded

a leap of faith off the bridge to everywhere

a forever burning candle in the scent of burnt offerings

love is hard and soft a circle with jagged corners

a square with round edges

an ocean covered in white sands

a beach with a lake front view

I have learned firsthand

hearts come equipped with its own fingers

able to choose its recipient with out our participation

at first glance I was not aware of what you are to me

eyes will never be the determining factor

of beauty in real life

she walked as if her feet hurt

from treading broken hearts, shattered memories

or sharp pieces of lost loves

I had to tell her the truth

in the beginning was the word

I've heard it was a poem about you

there are commandments I have pledged to keep

remember the sabbath day

and keep it holy

every day with you are my sabbath

oh how I worship at your temple

you are the magnificent structure

sent me by the most high to cherish

you are why many believe there is gold

at the end of rainbows

why in the days of old men wore six shooters

you are the secret treasure hidden in pyramids

why butterflies are beautiful

your smile smells of Gods breath

I know he talks of me sometimes

how I miss you when we sleep

how you are the gift in every fantasy

the prize in my celebrations

did he tell you every prayer I pray

begins with your name

we only talk about you whenever we speak

there are details I asked him to keep to himself

Not Just Alphabets

Steel Black

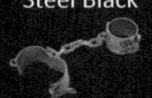

heaven knows we do not do secrets

there are clouds filled with tears of joy

so when it rains – I shared those with you

I have followed you

thousands of miles from home

your eyes are the locks and keys

to every place I want to live

your legs go from earth to stars

as if that eternity is where I need to be

I started believing in ghosts last night

felt you caress my body

as a Tyrannosaurus Rex would

if their arms were longer

I could hear the song you sang months ago

still playing in Heaven as if you are their playlist

you haunt me as if ordained or chosen

you stay as close as sound or air

you are the air I need for sustenance

felt you kiss the inside of my lips

you were on your way-out

as though your soul resides in the core of me

she arrived locked and loaded

wasn't prepared to give more than a smile

missions are not mysteries

we knew we were meant to be

love has led is here

neither of us will be leaving soon

could be we mapped love into a galaxy

we are planets in motion orbiting hearts

an astrological phenomenon

the sharp in the blade of a warrior

the prayers in the knees of children

asking for a miracle

we are miracles in the brushes of painters

framing forever in the canvas of time

it is written in the beginning was the word

it has always been a poem about you

Steel Black

Monuments

I keep grasping at pens

not for sure I can build

this message out of ink

sometimes ink is not the best material

for constructing anything everlasting

what if we measured words like horses

how many hands did it take for you to write it

we have been her before - plenty of times

but not once with our fist raised

not once with a message we can harmonize

one we can grow our children to

stop repeating words not worth the sound

or breath used to create them

I keep hearing King, Lewis, Malcolm

Attucks, Barack, my father

yelling

do not walk on the water - it is not drinkable

the chemicals will make your skin fall off

those fish cannot fry, can't bake, won't die

shut them rocks up that keep crying out

how you gone be you

when you keep walking

in other people shoes

watch how high you climb

that mountain it is full of landmines

there are few safe places

for dreamers, this ain't one

I keep reaching for the mic

and it's not my turn

no time to listen to logic

can't hear truth while they still dance

while they keep playing songs

with no message, can you tweet

twerk, Facebook, Instagram Live

Tic Tock what you want to say

maybe then you will be placed in rotation

I wanted to write something

I could give to you for free

something you would be willing to pay for

it would be worth more than your time and money

something you would share with those you care about

today we need to care for more than just ourselves

I wrote a poem out of steel, out of lead, out of clouds

I wanted it to be heavy enough

Not Just Alphabets

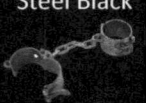

Steel Black

you could not carry it by yourself

you would need help to lift the thoughts

between the lines

you would be willing to read it right now

not wait till tomorrow

I keep grasping at straws

you know, the ones that broke the camel's back

maybe if there were dust enough

you would know how rough it is to stay tough

when all you have left is empty promises

when all your poems are ten hands tall

none of your pens have saddles

reigns or blinders

only hair triggers no safety

won't stay within the borders you forced them live

I wanted to build a poem, a monument

that would stand in your way

beautifully constructed as if it fell from heaven

you would have to take the long path around or drive by

it would distract you from doing

all the nothings you find yourself participating in

it would be loud and quiet

bright and dark written in every language

it would be filled with footholds, handrails

hidden drawers for wings and trumpets

there would be drums with harp strings

flutes with wind chimes - free halo's

ink puddles you can stand in

I need to write a poem

the likes of which you've never heard

and will never hear again

I want to build a poem out of skin and bones

with bright white teeth

unaffected by time unafraid of Covid

a poem you can dance to, rock with

one able to harmonize on its own

a poem that comes with

its own pen and paper

its own directions on how to read it

how to go from back to front

from side to side

one that will explain itself

without anyone asking

will not let you finish writing it

no matter how many times you stop

you know that poem

Steel Black

like the straw

that broke the camel's back

like the cow

still hanging on that corner

of a crested quarter moon

that poem, you know

you can lead a poet to paper

but you can't make poets write

you know

yeah, that poem

No Not One

I stood in awe

imagining a multitude of slaves

hands muddy, fingers moving

working together to form each shingle

placing them side by side

building the first black owned church

this was the first piece of real estate America

allowed any dark skin person or group to own

in 1758 there are no mysteries when history

deletes part of itself on purpose

there will be truths we are always learning

always finding behind locked doors and pages

you may have to travel beyond the walls

of your present domicile to discover

at the completion of my tour of Whitley Plantation

there were two branches unevenly broken

resting on the bench as if they knew

upon departure I would pass this way

they sat there knowing I did not know

which tree they freed themselves from

why this time, right here, right now

Steel Black

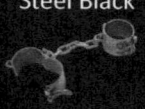

they needed me to notice them

maybe these small branches had grown tired

of holding centuries of bad memories

tired of clinging to a tree growing roots of remorse

too many years of sorrow, of sadness

with more than a century of regret

could be just now they gave up living

wanted to make me aware of their troubles

even nature will give up when pain

reaches the point of being too much to bear

they are the only ones who knew

who heard the screams, the cries

felt the blood dripping down its trunk

the only ones who knew how many bodies

are planted here, unable to find peace

without lips they cannot tell the whole story

can only share it in pieces in leaves

my heart paused after entering the church

on pews, in corners, standing as ushers

in the choir stand were the statues

of little black children waiting

eyes hollowed they too have seen

too much hurt, too much blood

too much trouble to share

cried soo many tears

they removed their eyes

how many times

can we watch the destruction

of individuals, of a people, of a culture

the posting of videos of police brutality

the murder of innocent, the harassment

of individuals minding their own business

there will be times human suffrage

will make us wish to remove our eyes

how can two broken branches tell the story

history keep refusing to remember

someone must take pains dictation

write memories direct refusal

we cannot forget

we will forever be learning truths

hidden on purpose

we were never meant to find

Not Just Alphabets

Steel Black

Sunshine and Rain

before computers

before the inception

of the internet, before stamps

before western union

before Ma Bell, before horseless carriages

we misidentified the connection between

plantation and president

congress and overseer

before we knew anything

of pall and bearers

long before we met the twins

Cem and Tary our eternal question

has been how come Justice

every time she is birthed, reformed of pain

or rebirthed must be blind, blindfold or not

cannot see beyond the paleness of her skin

beyond declaring of our captivity

or rather our undependence

you see they wrote about us, or is that

unwrote about us in America's scriptures

America got pages of which we are not included

not referenced, no free

no liberty, maybe death

history is a land mine

filled with broken promises

a stuttered voicemail

repeated in thunder

from the clouds

an attempt to clear a ruptured

past hoping to insure the possibility

the slimmest of slim chances

if we listen close enough

we will find a way

a trail of breadcrumbs

loss footsteps in the wind

a guide that will lead us to take a step

or two forward although backward

be the preferred direction

there are fields of scattered nightmares

and dreams tossed about on unfertile soil

on purpose, the only thing

we are able to grow

are headstones

we plant enough of them

Steel Black

around this great country

every week we plant one of our seeds

more than six feet deep

imagine time delivered us

a box of problems

a thirteenth commandment

at least twelve dozen cases of regret

stamped return to sender

no one knows its origin

or where they came from

they keep asking me

to write a good poem

of happy, find some jovial

locate that two step

a glorious pair of them Shirley Temple

and Bill Bojangles shoes

dances we have yet

to recover from

keep asking me to write a poem

fill it with smiles

from a darkened history

that has remained black

long after the sun came out

we have experienced at least

one hundred and ten thousand

appearances of the sun and still can't

see a clear day

a day without a storm

in one of our communities

without a dark cloud over the house

of some innocent person

no longer with us

bet they can't fathom

how we keep moving

how we keep picking up bodies

and tombstones and memories

carrying them with us

time has left scars we are afraid

to look at

cannot remember

where they came from

Steel Black

What Hate Looks Like

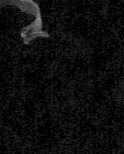

these days I paint my pictures

spit these verses

write these lines with a harness attached

to the clip of my pen

no one really knows how hard it gets

to control the uncontrollable

sometimes your life, these lines

a poem will force you to place

a seatbelt around your fingers

a parachute or a pressure plate

underneath your tongue

even the bible tells us of the power of words

you may be required to walk on air

clouds or water, tiptoe across

the last two bridges you burned

from sky to dirt just to get back that you

you had no idea where you last saw yourself

I got mirrors that quit being mirrors

a long long time ago

You don't know how you see yourself

until you really see yourself

for years your shadow has been

embarrassed to tag along

your feet do not like living side by side

no longer leave footprints in the mud

you will never know what problems are

until you have an ex be it wife or girlfriend

that believes you owe them everything

everything you got or hope is coming

for the rest of your life

I know now that's what hate looks like

when you've paid child support for 30 years

and Texas demands you owe an additional

30 years as if the state is still angry

at General Granger who arrived

robbed them and disrupted

their ability for free labor

I believed only America would dig

that deep into the past

and force you to pay for it

with your future, asking for every one

of your tomorrows that ain't here yet

good thing I don't have my father's tongue

and heaven blessed me with my mother's love

Steel Black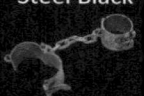

The Air They Un Promised Us

we were promised air or breath

pursuit of happiness, liberty

equality and justice for all

we believed they were all included

I think it was in the preamble or one of those

documents with added amendments

written on hemp or just old paper

could be it was directly implied

or merely inferred

it seems it was unpromised

when there was no justice offered

for the assassinations of black leaders

labeled enemy number one and troublemaker

when important provisions of the civil rights act

were removed by the supreme Court

when regulators were not for sure if choke holds

by the police should be banned

if knees should be considered weapons

when stray bullets did not have

to be accounted for

when death resulted by

no knock warrants are overlooked

when videos fail to be

considered verifiable proof

when statements by eyewitnesses

can only be taken

if your skin is not the color of oppression

like every tribe of American Indian

we have grown use to broken promises

never knew promises could be kept

thought they were contracts

agreements, treaties

America's record is impeccable

when it comes to her word

even when written or read out loud

it is not worth the sound created

or the paper it is printed on

America is better at unpromising

so much better at the fingers crossed

eyes crossed, toes crossed handshake

the up and down nod in opposition

the too small font unreadable fine print

America has no memory of the last time

or the first time she kept a promise

Steel Black

Muddy Water

I grew up thinking muddy water

were what little boys

played in when it rained

each time it rained

in play clothes or Sunday's best

I played, jumped, splashed

and ran through muddy water

did not matter how many times

I was told not to

there had to be something in my DNA

making me want to remember

demanding I never forget

it is frightening how knowledge can change

literally the way your eyes view the world

when I learned no one knew how many

exactly where, which coast, which shore

those free men and women chained together

leaped into the ocean

they would not go into the night

not be bound and forced into ships

on a mission to places unknown

together they had enough faith

in whatever god you think they knew

believing without a doubt

give me free or else

I will not let you take me away from this place

away from everything I know

this land is sacred the world was birthed here

as a child I never thought

muddy waters could be so thick

so heavy with burdens it will not

allow me to write them

words can't spell, can't mean

can't translate, can't equal

what was taken, what was lost

what we still search for

every time it rains, I drag

my fingers through muddy waters

praying I find what my soul is searching for

what we lost in the ocean chained together

with belief so powerful, I wonder

were they conscious when they

made it to the bottom

what conversations were shared

Steel Black

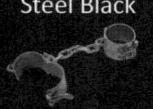

before breath ran out

this had to be the first time

a group of people yelled

to whatever god resides above those clouds

I Can't Breathe, give me

freedom or give me death

America changed the freedom to liberty

we still wait for their interpretation

it does not mean

what is defined in dictionaries

muddy waters have taken

so many alternate meanings

for decades police have planted

whatever they felt necessary

to get a conviction

in cars, closets, houses, on persons

our community is full of muddy water

from judges paid to fill cells for profit

from DA's scapegoating innocence for guilty

we have served concurrently centuries of time

decades upon decades of muddied waters

even when found innocent courts refuse to comply

how muddy does the water have to be

for us to see it has never been drinkable

McKinley Morganfield, Muddy Waters, post war blues

was music before his time, maybe like me he searched

for answers in muddy waters

ran his fingers through puddles each time it rained

had questions about breath and breathing

wondered how or where the footprints came from

some nights, pillows drenched in sweat

I dream it rained, a revolution, a massive downpour

there are always footprints in the places no one has tread

leading me away from wherever I thought I was

to where I need to be - it is never the same place

there is always mud, always water, always footprints

none are mine, they resemble the child I was

when my parents told me not to play in puddles

the prints are the same size mine used to be

accompanied by a much bigger dream

I wonder if souls buried on ocean floors

can be transported through muddy waters

to everywhere on this globe

can speak to the living, how do your messages appear

I need to know where these voices come from

dancing in my head, who leaves these footprints

Steel Black

what language speaks in fluent ink

what god would use muddy water to pass a message

to teach a heathen how to pray in poems

to hear lessons in the rain

repeating the same refrain from ocean floors long ago

by groups of people too proud to give up

it was the first time a chorus sang, screamed

and yelled to whatever god resides above those clouds

I Can't Breathe, give me freedom or give me death

America changed freedom to liberty

we are still waiting for the proper clarification

Crowns

I would never ask

where did it come from

if she bought it on discount

is it made in child labor camps

I know real is on the package

because it is touchable

but is it real

does it feel of yarn, mane or human

I would never ask these questions

no matter how frequently

they show up on the tip of my tongue

no matter if the hair is purple

orange, green, blonde, long, short

doesn't cover your roots, sit crooked

I would think maybe your head has a slant

I would never ask any of the necessary questions

to make me understand why you chose to place

such a contraption on your crown

is it royal, does it come with perks

do peasants bow when they greet you

does it bear medicinal qualities

Steel Black

of which I am simply unaware

now tell me why you touch mine

when I am not looking

ask if it's real

as if this isn't the way

Jah planned

how did I place the gray

so strategically perfect

how long have we been dating

how many years have we been friends

how old is each loc

there is a reason most of us

are born bald to give each of us time

to adjust to the crown we are given

nappy – straight – curly

black – blonde – brown

you were gifted what you got

this is how my hair is supposed to be

like Enoch, Sampson and Jesus the Nazarite

a crown is a crown is a crown

wear yours with pride

yours was gifted at birth

it is yours for a reason

We The People

I know why the police keep stopping us

why every time we are out in this American air

they do not see us as individuals as persons

we are surrounded by ancestors protecting us

for mere spectators they see us the one, as many

cannot tell us apart from them that got stopped before us

from them that got stopped before them

from them that got caught, from them that jumped

could not give up free for hope of some new shore

praying they could breathe underwater

did not know liberty or death

but death be liberty for some

they keep re catching us as if they sense

how hard it is for free to attach itself to these bones

It is easy to see how free looks pasted on dark skin

visible on the outside as if white free on black skin

could remain invisible, continue to be undetectable

hiding free under your tongue will make you stutter

simulate a speech impediment

we keep attempting to write us free

through whatever means or methods necessary

Steel Black

they keep taking it back

keep rereading the constitution

knowing we ain't whole, knowing

you can't attach rights to three fifths of a person

knowing we got issues with declarations

with old papers and white signatures

with white men bearing good tidings, wigs on tight

knowing we have been written out of documents

after a show of hands or votes forced you to pencil us in

to write us partial, as portions of a person

cannot tell you how free keep falling out of them cuts

from old buffalo whips too many years ago

out of them bullet holes

in our backs from traffic stops

the villain forever free

still puts on blue every morning

it has been that way for centuries

maybe not dressed in confederate blue but white

eyes cut out for a hat we call a hood

one hundred thread cotton

just like our ancestors picked

like the struggles of men and women

daily trying to get that bale of white gold

even back then they called them peace officers

ain't no peace when they come to our hood

got nothing but war, prejudice and pain on they brain

too many of them got Jim crow stuck in their teeth

some of them got Massah's foot on their right leg

Uncle Tom and Barry Goldwater in them palms

George Wallace tattoos hidden up their sleeve

dressed in them Willie Lynch pants

heard long time ago Willie only wore blue too

same as confederates, same as police

I know why they keep stopping us

wanting to search our backpacks search our souls

make sure we ain't carrying some of Moses

miles to get us free

a lot of us got some of that Attucks in our veins

they can hear all that Malcom leaking out of our throats

all chickens coming home and any means necessary

know we got Bobby Hayes and Jim Brown in our legs

they know they can't catch us if we run

that is where lead come in, bullets have the unique ability

to keep us down, keep us under the dirt

history has proven how hard it is for niggaz to fly

with his back filled with lead or a rope around his neck

Steel Black

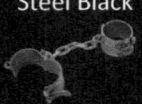

Initially the intent was not to kill us

they could not stand how we looked all dressed up

in that free that kept promising we could keep

America too used to taking back promises

regifting temporary land and sample freedom to us

to them that owned this dirt before sticking a flag

in the ground became proof of ownership

America real good at rewriting the bad they done, good

making cowards into heroes, building traitors

ten feet tall, they will Edison your invention

long before the ink on the patent dry

the cacophony of caskets without names

is a matter we need to speak on

how shallow graves is a real thing

bodies whose bones

lay just above the second layer of sand

we got communities literally built on the backs

of our ancestors and wonder why we cannot sleep

the only reason I can see through the haze

this poison filtered water keep our left eye blurred

I got Jimmie Jay pupils, been learning white etiquette

like he taught me, like he showed me

we the people of these un united states

it was made impossible for us to form

a common union no justice in our communities

no peace on our streets

three fifths may be right we have yet to act

as if we are whole, how many years removed

must we be removed before we make ourselves

make our communities whole

what if we found some Martin in our soles

a little Ghandi in our hearts how many more

of us need to kill us before we wake up

before we write a bill of rights for Black Communities

a constitution that works, before we discover

it is up to us to dig us out or dig us dipper

every time we step out in this American air

we are surrounded by ancestors trying to keep us safe

attempting to protect us mainly from ourselves

Steel Black

Home

somedays you will find it is the dirt we call home

not the house, hood, city, not the block or borough

I keep trying to discover how unity works

why a people upon arrival chained together

can no longer find a connection, cannot remember how it felt

to be family, to share the same darkness, same pain

wish I knew why this dark skin is not an identifier of brotherhood

used to be a raised fist was enough to make us kindred

cannot figure out how we have been listening for centuries

and still cannot hear the message, cannot make out words left for us

cannot translate a language our tongue should easily be able

to understand, tell me why clicks don't make sounds

why young men with the same skin must still choose a color

why have we become better repeaters of tradition than truth

how neighborhoods disappeared with people still living there

remember when house parties played music, homes were

filled with entertainment and laughter did not have

a nine-millimeter, forty-five or clock soundtrack exploding

in the background, how come common ground has nothing

to do with sand, followers has nothing to do with feet

likes has little to do with friendship or liking someone

why brother or sister do not always mean blood

mom and dad do not have to equal seed

there are so many things I do not know

wish there were clues, a ledger

a road or pirate's map, a newfound way to discover

how ancestors got us this far without cellphones or internet

how did we forget how to listen and why listening is necessary

we lack the skills and intelligence to do what they did

lack the follow through to make nineteen trips over ten years

more than eight hundred miles each to give freedom

to a group of people we have never met

and don't know, we keep forgetting

this ain't home

this is the land, the place, could be the second or third stop

on a mission to be sold as livestock, linked together

as if we were already property, already paid for

bought and sold by kings and queens, by nations

by countries who did not think this skin had worth

this can't be home

this dirt doesn't feel welcoming

makes my feet hurt, don't taste like children should play in it

I believe they have been shooting craps and playing scabble

with our bones for as long as we have been here

Steel Black

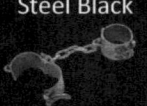

this ain't home

there are broken links to old-rusted chains

and shackles lying on every beach in the south

those are not random planks on the shores of the east

those are remnants of ships used to transport slaves

ashamed of their participation, embarrassed

history left their names intact, who knows the length

of the memory of trees now they can't leave

spirits are holding them captive, keeping them bound

to America's shores like slavery, like property

like they did us, those are not state or government lands

being used for hydraulic fracturing and drilling oil

those are sacred Indigenous burial grounds ravaged

stolen, those are lands of broken treaties

where promises were shattered on purpose

this country refuses to acknowledge its part

in the disciplined annihilation of Indian tribes

the systematic racism of the once enslaved

the planned and scheduled incarceration

of dark-skinned boys starting in the third grade

this ain't home

when imminent domain can instantly uproot your comfort

when hiked up taxes can render you homeless

when being black can render you target

deliver you to your parents breathless

your police killer go free, no charges

how can home be where the heart is

when America remains heartless

this country charges us fees to explain

how many granules of foreign dirt

makes up our feet, how many pieces

of our jigsaw puzzled DNA compiles this skin

how far we must go to find family

how many countries it will take make us whole

this ain't home

I doubt America wants it to be

at the rate they are retuning us to dirt

home has nothing to do with structures

has everything to do with earth

we do not know where home is

this dirt is not kind

does not greet my feet as if I am welcome

only holds my body hostage after brutality

after beatings, after bullets

after hate takes our last breath

maybe then, this will be home

Not Just Alphabets

Steel Black

Unforgiven

in grade school I was taught things

I am ashamed for remembering

as an adult I read the stories found in

so called history books most should be labeled

children's tales, written or painted

on canvases in pixie dust

the telltale beginning with a hero heading

of the captain's name

followed by the name of the ship

identifying ocean an embellished declaration

of treacherous weather

experienced on a mission of discovery

I have never understood why upon arrival

finding whatever space discovered already inhabited

has been for longer than the land you came from

none of the supposed explorers found it in their heart

to leave, create a map for others on similar pursuits

declaring these lands already taken

this country was rediscovered on a mission

to find a place to experience religious freedoms

which religion, what God would allow you

to exterminate any race of people

what religion could authorize you

the freedom to rape and pillage

in such barbaric fashion

why are you on your knees

who are you looking up to

why close your eyes, no higher power

would condone this behavior

would not strike you crippled

I tried to make a list of America's atrocities

America's mistreatment of mankind

the who, what, when, where, how's

the harrowing history of American oppression

actually begins with America, starting with captains

settlers, Chris, pilgrims, contracts, agreements, treaties

the declaration of undependence, the afterAmble,

lady liberty should be equipped with lights as a warning

red and blue in color, sirens, explosions as if we are

forever looking at the dawns early light, ramparts

and streamings, I have tried to forget unthanksgivings

slave owner presidents' birthdays, black leader

assassination holidays, traitor day as if confederate

generals would be celebrated in any other country

Steel Black

I keep asking myself what is forgiving

how does it work, I used to live

two houses from the corner

on the other side of town

from where the ships arrived

I had friends that spoke Spanish

even then I didn't understand

run, hide, the British - I mean ICE is coming

I understood run, hide those are the words we use daily

trouble in our communities arrive dressed in two colors

either blue or black, troubles never start at harvest

doesn't show up when you GPS your destination

troubles start at birth, at inadequate hospitals

at less than minimum waged jobs

troubles begin when bus routes

won't get you all the way to work

will fail to take you all the way home

you will not understand what trouble is

Until, your skin contains melanin

you speak a language considered foreign

by American standards

your eye color is anything but blue

I am ashamed for teaching my children

the misinformation, the direct and blatant

false stories America carved into books

then labeled it history, I cannot recall

America apologizing with sincerity

asking all these generations of people

all the nationalities still residing

in accompanying islands, states, districts

to forgive them for centuries of misdeeds

of ill will, I guess she, America

will remain unforgiven, will keep

the bloodstains on her flag

police uniforms, judges robes

court documents, stock market trades

currency

I am not sure how forgiving works

I just know

you cannot continue to do the things

you are asking

to be forgiven for

Not Just Alphabets

Steel Black

Rise

life is filled with test

we either pass or fail

each one of us practiced taking them

after we attended school

in order to graduate as a senior

we needed to have the right answers

to receive our cap and gown

what no one explained to us

those were all the easiest test

filled with easy answers, you could turn pages

and find solutions, real life will never appear on pages

there are no books in which to find the answers

every day there are test we will pass or fail

we were not aware any of these were test

they came to us as trials, although we never knew

they were coming, when reading of the life of Job

his were not test they were examples

you can lose everything for no reason

most will claim you deserved it

Job recovered more than he lost

Job was the test to teach us a lesson

we know nothing of the life of Lazarus

there is no record of him being good or bad

we don't know if he passed or failed his test

all we know is someone prayed, begged

ask God to bring their brother back

we know the rest of the story

do you know how many people

prayed for you, every night on bended knees

how many tears were shed for your resurrection

begged God to bring their sister back

you, me all of us here are Lazarus

no one needs to know the life you lived before

the test you didn't pass, the trials you failed

they can see you have come back

risen from the tomb of despair

you, me all of us here are Lazarus

with Job like qualities blessed to be here

we can tell the story of how we overcame

of rising from the ashes, of the glory of being

blessed, for we are all blessed...

there are hallelujahs in being resurrected

in being renewed - in rising like Lazarus

we are here for a reason

Steel Black

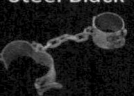

these tears we cry were given us to shed

the hugs we give are filled with prayers

my knees are scarred from talking to God

I told him about you

asked him to erase your history with drugs

begged him to replace your cravings with love

you, me, we are all Lazarus

resurrected from the ashes of addiction

Life is filled with test we either passed or fail

we've been given the answers

a new beginning with a chance at glory

these tears are ours to share

these hugs are filled with prayers

and this is an I love you from me

there is beauty in being blessed

in receiving a second chance

you, me all of us here are Lazarus

rise - remember where you came from

how hard it was to get here

the struggle you must go through to stay

you, me all of us here are Lazarus

rise, reclaim your life, discover the glory of living

Rise!

This Is Why Death Sounds So Familiar III

today's breaking news sounded as if

it was written yesterday or last year

in 1990, 1985, 1972, 1620

breaking news stopped breaking

the minute caution tape became

the only thing holding our communities together

the only thing we use to keep our pants up

when gunshots became the only way

we communicate

breaking news stopped breaking

when posters on city walls explained

where the next auction would be held

described the content of the next slave ship

what time the next hanging is taking place

bring your children and a pic nic basket

we will be here for a minute

you wonder why no one speaks

when shots are fired

why no one sings negro spirituals at funerals

why black is not the required color

when we escort boxes to graveyards

Steel Black

we've gotten so used to burying us

no invitation is sent out

we just arrive on time

week after week we arrive on time

you wonder why death sounds so familiar

it's because we kill us more than they kill us

remorse is a transmission in beeps, in clicks

a code used during war time

and believe me - this is war time

Imagination and Apologies

I keep forgetting

every page begins as breath

some part of a tree

always saving our lives

I used to offer an apology

before I began

sketching one word

a line or thought

treated every page with reverence

two Amen and five hail Mary's

where did the grateful go

how come I am sorry's

are so hard to come by

I can only imagine we have become

lost in days, trapped in moments

that have grown cumbersome

capsules of time we are unable

to write ourselves out of

forget what you have been told

imaginations cannot grow

they will forever remain

Steel Black

the same size they were

the instant we discovered

the power of painting

our thoughts in verses

you ask me to convert

apologies into imagination

what if every apology is built

of seeds from our imagination

Be Careful

when my father told me

be careful

I thought it was just something

fathers say to their sons

I didn't know he meant

'be careful'

I'm guessing he knew

my heart wasn't completely attached

could have heard it rattle around

or maybe the doctors warned him

before I left the hospital

must have seen traits as a child

love wouldn't be kind to the man I'd become

I am just hearing his words now

'be careful'

if I would have listened

where would I be right now

after loving the wrong people

giving too much of myself

to those with slippery fingers

beautiful faces with wondering eyes

Steel Black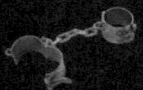

women unable to keep their hands

to themselves

be careful

had to be the statement he meant it to be

I wish my ears had a time capsule

had vise grips for fingers

our ability to listen

has nothing to do with sound

or understanding, wanting

needing, or our ability to love

we were not born knowing

or believing - love was something

we needed to be careful about

I wish my father were here

I would tell him how you arrived

careful

how soft your feet greeted the earth

how your legs move in perfect harmony

how you knew

you knew what he told me

how did you know

did he tell you too

Envy

I was never really impressed

with the moons sacred dance with night

or stars waiting until we look up

to shoot across the sky

did you know they've been dead

for a length of time we could never measure

I am not envious of how typhoons

show up without notification

or why clouds calypso, twirl and spin

into tornadoes or hurricanes and oceans

although enemies

sometimes hang like family

if I envy anything, I envy you

I wish to be the delicate grace

the patience of immortals

the slow hand heaven used

to create you, I could never envy love

you came with extra hearts

an abundance of caring

if I envy anything, I envy you

how you have withstood

Steel Black

the un with stand able

how the wind tries to smile

like you if we could see it

how prayers ask for you by name

how butterflies wish to paint

enough colors on their wings to garner

your glance, you have shown me

the sky has corners

galaxies have limits and imagination is

everything we need to build a new

if I envy anything, I envy you

for reasons I could never pen and paper

will never accept, I envy you

Play Me Some Jazz

when she spoke it was music

made my heart dance as if beats wore feet

some days I sat back just to listen

I would whisper in her ear, play me some jazz

the way she walked was an upright bass

her smile a cello with a host of tenor saxophones

painting background

she whispered in violins with a hint of oboe

how can anyone be as beautiful as notes

she was sheet music if ever sheets could play music

often, I wait until right past midnight

whisper softly in her ear - play me some jazz

she smiles as if angels sat gracefully

in the corners of her lips

her eyes were a string section

complete with xylophone and harp

her caress was as soft as a viola or piccolo

able to touch ears and hearts at the same time

she was every instrument you could imagine

she was a Billie Holiday melody with an

Ella Fitzgerald scat a Sarah Vaughan song

Steel Black

sung by Nina Simone and Aretha Franklin

She was jazz personified

music encased in the most beautiful skin

she was hum and chorus the lead legs

in your favorite opera

she was jazz whenever I asked

always played in the perfect melody of love

she is the perfect melody of love

now every day I ask her in whispers

play me some jazz

Speaker Tax

(Free Speech Ain't Free)

maybe you want to know what happened

how truth no longer equals truth

this

this be that message in a bottle

the three rubs on Aladdin's lamp

the key to Pandora's box

the footprints in the sand

at the bottom of the ocean

on the edge of the cliff

on the ledge of dirty minds

this be that letter with no stamp

returned to sender free of charge

if free speech is free

it is sound that has a levy

it is going to cost you to listen

I got some shit you need to hear

there is a speaker tax on this voice

truth doesn't come with refunds

there is a toll tax a soul tax

on the imagination of writers

Steel Black

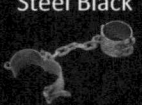

it is not necessary to repeat silence

when you already heard the sound

to call truth inconvenient you need to know

whose number you are dialing

with whom you are speaking

the original source of information

we got breaking news that ain't breaking

some of the messengers sent

came on their own

all their messages

they made that shit up

maybe you want to know what happened

how truth no longer equals truth

I got a pocket full of solutions

to problems that have not been found yet

some prayers forgot to put their hands together

are still stuck on the tips of tongues

can't be shared when your knees

are this scarred

some days it gets too hard to teach

sometimes I can't remember

what language god speaks

this

this is that storm

showing up with no warning

that house fire from bad wires

that gas leak that blew up

the whole block

this is the lightning strike

that set the forest ablaze

this is the language god speaks

lies cost more than truth

that should be easy to see

simplicity is like a truce to me

you used to share your truth with me

sound ain't what it used to be

you use your ears so selfishly

talk angry like we got some beef

you rattle like you losing teeth

this poetry ain't no trick or treat

there is no beat no hook to repeat

cover your ears to stop the leaks

honor every tree that gave us sheets

and know ain't no free

in freedom of speech

Steel Black

The Messenger
(Birth Write)

America used to have questions

not all answers

it would ask, it is ten PM

do you know where your children are

since then we have lost a lot of our children

not just lost, murdered, killed, missing

I was born with a message in my mouth

a two-tablet tongue too heavy to lift sound

two commandments I can remember

listen while you can

learn everything possible

knowledge is the type of explosion

with the potential of mass mental excavation

you can never be too careful

it is my birth write before I could write, right

some messages take time to translate

it maybe your job to construct them

from the damage, destruction, devastation

from the carnage left after reconstruction

tell them! statues erected years after treason

cannot produce a hero out of stone

they will keep changing the story

attempting to give history

a much needed make over

God / Jah told me to tell you

He expects more out of you

than you have put forth

He has so much in store for you

much more than you could ever imagine

you cannot take your time

because no time is yours

yours is on loan you have to return it soon

your purpose will not wait

it has the authority to leave

if fail to pay attention

wishes are the beginning steps

in an all-out sprint

you must practice wishing

before you try to walk

running is unnecessary when your path

has already been ordered

dreams were miss named

they should have remained wants

Steel Black

then you would know dreams

don't have wings

cannot take you up or down

cannot transport you to better

worse will be here before you realize

you had so many others places

you were supposed to be

jogging in place is as useless

as a shower with no water

standing still and waiting for whatever

you think you're waiting for will get you lost

move while you listen

learn to do at least two things at once

there is legacy in your feet

there were a million miles on them

before you discovered how they worked

never take walking or marching for granted

tongue tied means you have never studied

the proper use of sounds

learn to listen

watch what you say

with the movement of your life

many will speak of doing and not do

talk of building with no tools

say I love you with likes

I was born with a message

too often the messenger

will not take time to read

think it is not for him or her

learn to read first

do not forget to learn to listen

being a messenger will not absolve you

of the duty you have been given

your purpose can leave

if you fail to pay attention

you have a duty to yourself to be the best you

to find that good you have been searching for

there is more good in you than you realize

in the beginning my lips were not strong enough

did not have strength of lungs to make you believe

this message is for you

you stopped listening to your conscious

when it rebelled against your dreams

your wants - you think tomorrow

is the perfect answer to every question

that comes your way

Not Just Alphabets

Steel Black

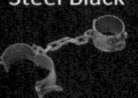

you have a duty to not wait

time is not yours, do not forget your clock

is on loan you will be obligated to return it soon

greatness does not do selfies

does not know who you are

doesn't care what you post

how many friends, acquaintances

I mean followers you have

life happens in real time

no replay, is not streamed many think I am mad

I was born with a message

a two-tablet tongue too heavy to lift sound

no one told me how to give it, how to live it

should it be penned, yelled, spoken, poemed, sung

I don't know how you hear

but you better learn to listen

I was born with a message

God / Jah told me to tell you

He expects more out of you than you have put forth

No time is yours time does not belong to you

your purpose will not wait

it has the authority to leave

if fail to pay attention

Dear Martin, I Have a Dream

if we start with today and look back

as far as time will allow or history

will present us on pages

we can begin to compute how much we've paid

in this country to dream, if life

liberty and the pursuit of anything uncompromised

can be without prejudice

if black blood has an American equivalent

how the detachment of black body from breath

comes often with large donations

from the sheriff's department slush fund

as if they knew in advance you can only

determine the amount a black man is worth

once he is subtracted from his children

his family, once his mother cries foul

when his father rebukes the system

denounces the use of deadly force

once he can family no more

I wonder if Dr. King shows up in spirit

when called, when men, women and children

in any level of education repeat his speeches

Steel Black

when we call on him asking for a sign

is he aware we spent eight years

with a man that wore his same skin color

in the highest office in the nation

how can we get him a message to let

him know a minority woman will finally

have the honor of being Vice President

when is the last time he visited Ebenezer

his successor is following his footsteps

wears the title of first, first black senator

from the heart of dixie, I want to ask him

if he believed his words when he spoke

of character, of little black and white children

holding hands, if drum majors for justice

these days should carry long guns

there is no reason I should reference

the after effects of having A black president

no reason to discuss the last four years

in detail, promised myself I would not even

use twenty twenty in a sentence

would not say it out loud

would only write it in pencil

I would let him know klansmen

carry their guns, their rifles

in public, on government property

at least they leave their hoods at home

should I tell him they stormed the capital

the other day as if it was 1776 or 1876 again

they attempted to overthrow the government

you will not believe after all this time

they are finding new ways to steal

or cancel our vote, some republican secretary

of states randomly purge black voters

from the roll as if common place

others claim our votes should be discounted

because we voted at polling places

that were illegal, or mail in ballots

were not exactly authorized, if you came back

you would not be allowed to march

or even walk to view the mall

where you spoke to thousands, you could not

approach Lincoln's monument

would be forced to stand outside

the perimeter of a fence more than

seven feet in height, topped with razor wire

Lincoln could look down and believe

Not Just Alphabets

Steel Black

we were members of his plantation crew

finally America would be great again

Dear Martin it maybe worse

every time we take four steps up the ladder

to justice, they relocate the building

I wonder if you know how it looks

when the president of the United States

holds a rally to stop the count of electoral votes

how many confederate flags are in attendance

how many of the descendants

of good ole boys are still good ole boys

maybe our dreams are for sale

should be sold, or renewed

after every murder, after every

assassination, maybe we need

a lesson on mountain tops

Dear Dr. King I am not trying to

alarm you but here we may require

two of you and a couple of other leaders

in your recent acquaintance to come back

and teach master classes

especially since we be so close

to having masters again

Burdens

I recently discovered

the world of words I built

to rest my burdens

rested burdens only lay there

they never sleep

they don't know how

time is such a bad teacher

I would finger through them ever so often

their texture reminded me of you

not that you were ever burden to me

your newness feels old

like you've come back to visit

been here before

arrived

when I wasn't dressed to take you out

wasn't certified to care enough

these arms were not licensed

my heart was on sabbatical

it must have been the day

I discovered kisses

I knew how love was supposed to feel

Not Just Alphabets

Steel Black

and damn...

you feel like love

you have her eyes, those lips

probably feels like hers too

I built a world of words to hide my tears

the type of tears that will remain wet

longer than the memory forcing them

to rush from the corners of this face

words are much stronger

than their originator

than the thoughts they fell out of

it was you who pointed out in a song

words are great but you

damn

you are so much better than sound

than burdens resting on pillows of words

better than practicing getting ready

better than being ready to get ready

damn you have her eyes

I have always wanted to draw

wanted to sketch loves silhouette

place it on wanted posters

plaster it on the back of milk cartons

your lips probably feel like hers too

I built a world of words

you keep knocking down my alphabets

rearranging the structure of my sentences

got me trying to discover new ways to say

the simplest of thoughts

got me talking to myself

I knew how love feels

and damn

you feel like love

barely brushed your arm

felt your smile gently on my cheek

I built a bridge of words

knowing only you could see it

carved a map of longing

hoping you will use it to come home

Not Just Alphabets

Steel Black

Wide Open

imagine the beginning

ships landing on Plymouth Rock

more land than the lies they told

the language difference meant

they cannot own this wide open space

they arrived with nowhere else to go

crashed on these shores

as a last ditched effort to escape

these were not the good people

were not those of noble status

imagine all this space

all this wide open land

because of the language barrier

they cannot tell them it is theirs

they are not willing to give it up

on just a handshake, a short battle

a bottle of liquor, that fire water

what good is a treaty, any document

if they cannot understand

The language or the words written

in modern day America

America is still erasing lines

unshaking hands

most of the wide open spaces

have oil wells, pipelines

machines fracking

and drilling on hallowed ground

there are no more wide opens

it was flagged during the great migration

claimed, taken and given away for free

Steel Black

When I Grow Up

at the age of three I was writing

wrote in middle school, wrote plays

and poetry in high school

each time someone asked, my answer

was different than before

first it was singer, painter, architect

as a soldier I decided, when I grow up

I wanted to be a megaphone

a mountain top, a page, a pen

maybe the pen Martin held

the same one in the Lorraine Motel

setting in the drawer next to the bible

no one will open, or the pages that fell

from the podium after shots were fired

at the Audubon Ballroom

the stack of pages making up speech

Barack Obama read from as a senator

at the democratic national convention

I want to be the pen my mother used

to write the graceful blessings stored

in the hearts of family written in my

father's eulogy, when I grow up

I want to be the song Mahaila sung

"Take My Hand Precious Lord" at the

Request of Dr. King at his funeral

I want to be the memory of my sons

enabling them to recall how men are

supposed to be, how tall are mountains

when we consider them grown

when I grow up I want to be the light

sound creates, the darkness void of fear

I want to be doubt and fears reprieve

how much history can one man carry

how heavy are centuries of pain

I want to be times forgetfulness

histories lost memories, I want to be

hope, faith, I want to be love enough

for us all, a mountain made of hearts

hearts made of freedom

hearts with unity for hands

when I grow up I want to be the final poem

depicting America's hatred, the last poem

about unarmed black death, about pain

about absent fathers

Steel Black

about abandonment issues

when I grow up I want to be the poem

reciting hates and prejudices last rites

when I grow up let me be the best me

I can be, the sound solutions would make

If they had lips, an example of what

examples are supposed to look like

let me be love for all men carved

on pages in ink

They Make Me Nervous

once upon a time

I memorized all the books my mother

Had written by Dr. Suess

I found it easy to live imaginary to write

whatever I thought or dreamed

imagine telling your mother

at the age of five you are

a boy from Jupiter before anyone

ever told you of solar systems

little red, the three little, Peter Piper

fairytales make me nervous

how can you have more than two hundred

people gathered mask less during a pandemic

celebrating in the garden of Eden

and think the snake will not bite

the apple this time is not poison

it has to be a fairytale

how could any writer tell the story different

the tin man from Oz surrounded by secret service

waving from a protected limousine

in hospital gown, at innocent bystanders

Not Just Alphabets

Steel Black

voters, fans, a great while ago

when the world was full of wonder

there lived a man who ruled over a democratic nation

who wished to be king if insurrection

would allow, whose nose would grow

if the three thousand fables were correct

a long time ago so long no one can remember

so long there were no people, no dinosaurs

there were no trees, the rocks had not be given form

it is these times that make me nervous

I fear the masses ain't listening

fear the marchers will not just go home

the women will forget, the children from all the schools

with rooms filled with bullet holes for walls and windows

will stay home, I know November is a good

stones toss from here, sound doesn't last

as long as we think, I pray to heaven for

a pair of new knees, for poems to speak of

grace, for a time when rivers were made of hope

and wishes could come true

I pray for some truth tales, you know

it is the fairytales that make me nervous

End of the Road

I have never stopped to count

early estimates would be about 3000 poems

each a paved road destination unclear

my father taught me

there are only two things

I should fear, zigzag lightning

and the rath of God

here I stand at the end of this path

not wondering which way to go

but what poem can I write

to build a stronger bridge

a bridge from star to dust

from im to possible

I have a fine point pen

with angels trapped inside

I should let them free

I have written dreams heaven had to verify

their propensity or compute the exact ratio

of human comprehension, sometimes I write

to create things that are not even thoughts

as of yet, believe me that's all I know

Steel Black

America, I Am So So Sorry

this is not a poem

these are not words I wanted to write

had to force my pen to compose things

every pen I own refused to participate

writing in the beginning

I don't know how to explain history in a few words

do not know how to tell you how it feels

when America finally agrees

white supremacy, confederate flags

and their historical accompaniments

are all a horror story that has no place in this America

look how long it has taken for us to get to this point

America, I am so so sorry you had to watch

witness, experience firsthand representatives

senators, staff forced to hide in closets

under desk, behind locked doors

in safe rooms, heard them fervently praying to God

hands raised in sacred salutations pleading for salvation

asking Jesus, Allah for protection from American citizens

claiming their land, their country, their government

was taken, stolen, right from under their feet

I watched them pray, hands sweating

outstretched palms up as if white people

immediately began singing old negro spirituals

steal away, wade in the water, when I get to heaven

there was a time in our troubled past

these songs worked, got us here

torn and tattered, memories of pain but faith in tact

they were singing as if black Jesus or colored prayers

could get to heaven faster because we have been through

this sort of thing before, many times, this was their

first experience with attacks, hostile take overs

lynch mobs, white men and hate speech

America I am so so sorry you do not understand

how improper it is for white men to carry flags

in remembrance of prejudice, church burnings

murders, hangings, house bombings

how quick good ole boys throughout history

can erect gallows out of thin air

how the sons of good ole boys erected gallows

on capital property asking the vice president

speaker of the house to join their private celebration

America you should still have voicemails

from the first telephone ask Alexander Graham Bell

Steel Black

there should be records of telegraphs

from Samuel B Morse with help

please save us, the word emergency written

in capital letters, in big bold print

my great great grandfather never wanted to be

the one to say I told you so

my father although hinted a couple of times

did not want to say it either

I refuse to be the one saying I told you so

you must remember it has been said a million times

in the slave narratives, it was written in books

screamed from gallows, from underground

from ships, from fields, echoed from heaven

I refuse to be the one saying I told you so

America I am so so sorry

I wish you didn't have to face yourself facing yourself

wish you did not have to be afraid of people

with your same hue coming for you

wanting to rip apart your treasured constitution

wanting to devalue your bill of rights

even now you have not the slightest notion

which great again is being referenced

when the mob chants in unison

make America great again

who knew little white lies

could threaten your existence

as if you were black, I watched you

panic run terrified made me believe

you wore locs like me, I had to look again

to make sure your skin

did not have a permanent tan

do you realize they built fresh new gallows

outside of the capital, demanding

you disallow votes from people like me

wanted to teach you the justice

of the old days, none of them

willing to flow gently into that good night

for you there will be no more good nights

you like me will continue to look over

your shoulder, will remain at the ready

will know safety is only found

in the seatbelt of your car

who can predict the outcome when America

is finally afraid of America

I would hate to say I told you so

know this for sure I told you so

Steel Black

maybe you are praying

for the God of Abraham and Isaac

to smite them as if you finally believe

in the good and just treatment of all citizens

America I am so so sorry

you built this problem out of centuries of silence

out of corrupt court appointed attorneys

out of good old boy judges and police

I hate to say I told you so

this is not like before

when you fought yourself and begged

us to pick sides with the lie of free

we have been fighting for free

marching for some free

demanding you let us matter

but this time you are on your own

I apologize you failed to listen

but this time we are on our own side

America I am so so sorry

about the destruction of your norms

you did this to yourself

It is time for us to reread every moment of history we thought we knew. Every oral or written occurrence we read in magazines, newspapers or heard from those we trust. It is no fault of their own information has not always been verifiable, not always from a reputable source.

Thank you for your support, **Be Excellent**.

-aj houston-

Steel Black

Media Pages

http://www.instagram.com/ajwordartist

http://www.facebook.com/ajhoustom

http://www.twitter.com/ajwordartist

http://www.youttube.com/ajhouston

http://www.linkedin.com/ajhouston

https://www.amazon.com/AJ-Houston

http://www.ajhouston.blogspot.com

http://www.reverbnation.com/ajhouston

http://www.ajwordartist.wixsite.com/ajhouston

email: njalphabets@gmail.com

ajwordartist@gmail.com

Books Coming Soon

The Legend of Shrenk

Not Yet Lost

Lost Pens

The Fireplace

T - Shirts

Poetic Lessons

NJA Gear

ABOUT THE AUTHOR

AJ Houston is the son of Jimmie Jay and Birdie Lee Houston. He is the middle child with an older brother and sister and two younger sisters. He would say he has been a writer, poet all of his life. After memorizing all of the Dr. Suess books his mother read to him, he believed Dr. Suess created all of his characters from nothing, from thought. He spends his days with pen and paper attempting to discover his nothings to create everything from. "A poem should not say, but be." Is a quote from Ars Poetica gifted him by his high school English teacher, he has carried with him as a motto. One of his favorite quotes he has penned is, "if a picture is worth a thousand words each poem should be worth a thousand pictures". The description of writing and painting has to be the same process is the goal he offers to students in his create it writing classes. Creating a formidable follow through with everyday is his answer to anyone pouting writers block or being stuck in pause while writing. This is the ninth book published by Not Just Alphabets with the name AJ Houston as author. It is a privilege and a goal to publish enough books to be considered the author of his personal library, which would mean he has to publish at least 5 books a year. Thank you for the read, the follow if you clicked subscribe, follow, friend or whatever the media page requires. May we all be better stewards of the gifts we've been blessed with and may writing free your mind to dream bigger.

Not Just Alphabets

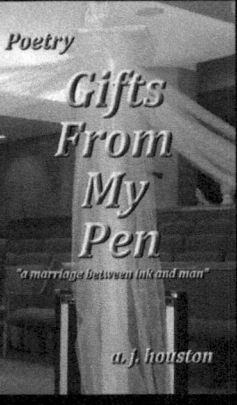
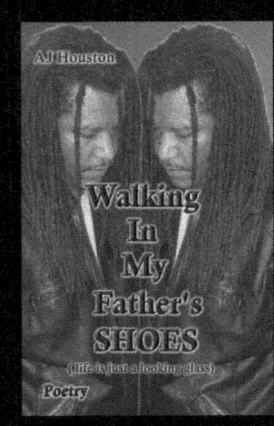
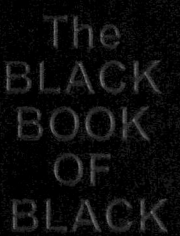
Steel Black

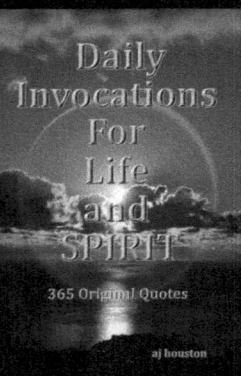

www.ingramcontent.com/pod-product-compliance
Lightning Source LLC
Chambersburg PA
CBHW050104170426
43198CB00014B/2450